Barrel of A Pen:

Resistance to Repression

in Neo-Colonial Kenya

Barrel of A Pen:

Resistance to Repression

in Neo-Colonial Kenya

Ngugi wa Thiong'o

Africa World Press
of the Africa Research & Publications Project

P.O. Box 1892
Trenton, New Jersey 08608

Barrel of A Pen: Resistance to Repression in Neo-Colonial Kenya
was first published by
AFRICA WORLD PRESS, P.O. Box 1892,
Trenton, N.J. 08608, USA (Worldwide except for:
Europe, West and Southern Africa and English
speaking Caribbean)

Cover Design by Ife Nii Owoo and an artist now residing in Kenya
who prefers to remain anonymous

Typeset by Tiffany Communications, New York

Layout: Carol Mitchell

Printed in the United States by Braun-Brumfield, Inc.,
Ann Arbor, Michigan

ISBN 0-86543-001-2 (cloth cover/cased)
ISBN 0-86543-002-0 (paperback)

Dedication

To Oginga Odinga, a great Kenyan, a great African, a great nationalist, now under house arrest for his life long struggle for the liberation of Kenya from colonialism and neo-colonialism, and for his uncompromising opposition to U.S. military bases and foreign troops in Kenya.

To George Anyona and Koigi-wa-Wamwere, two outspoken members of Parliament, now in detention without trial, for their consistent criticism of corruption and their principled struggle for the Kenyan poor.

To the six University lecturers: Al Amin Mazrui, Maina-wa-Kinyatti, Willy Mutunga, Kamoji Wachira, Edward Oyugi, Mucara Wg'any'a, now in prison and detention.

To all the students now in prison or awaiting trial for being the anti-imperialist and democratic conscience of Kenya.

To all the other political prisoners and all the Kenyans resisting the neo-colonial culture of silence and fear.

AND

To all those in and outside the country organizing and struggling for a new Kenya.

Contents

Preface

by Victoria Brittain *

The showpiece of British neocolonialism in East Africa is creaking under the strain of a bitter power struggle between competing factions of the elite, latent for years, and brought to crisis point by the mysterious and bloody coup attempt of August 1982. The in-fighting has critically undermined President Daniel Arap Moi himself and revealed how precarious his hold on power has been since he succeeded Jomo Kenyatta, Kenya's first president, in 1978. The channels of power in Kenya have always been narrow and personal revolving around a patron. The civilian entourage has now changed to include the army chiefs holding power behind the scenes.

A facade of "normality" has been thrown up in the months since August in an attempt to safeguard American strategic interests in East Africa and the Indian Ocean, and the Western business interests in Kenya. But Kenyans know that normality is a mere smokescreen. And they know too that only a government as profoundly alienated from its people as President Moi's could attempt a cover-up on the scale of the current one in Nairobi. Most Western diplomats have chosen not to penetrate the smokescreen. The regime's arrests and detentions weigh light against Western interests in "stability."

The government's death tally of 159 masks a grim reality which will never be counted accurately, but is estimated at 10 times that figure by doctors, priests, university lecturers who have seen mortuaries, mass graves, and distraught families whose children from the air force and the university have not been found dead or alive.

In the months since August 1 the conservative government has moved further to the right. This move to the right began earlier this year with a government campaign of repression of intellectuals which included detentions without trial, arrests on charges of possession of subversive literature, screening students for loyalty, and the seizing of passports to stem the trickle of intellectual exiles. It was a campaign to cripple the Kenyan left in every sphere. The university and the air force—the elite, educated wing of the armed forces—have been broken in the wake of the coup attempt so that they cannot recover under this regime or a related one. (The university has been closed and the air force disbanded.) At the same time, the government has unsuccessfully tried to pin the coup attempt on the Luo nationality from Western Kenya as a way of giving a tribal label to the mounting national opposition. The old nationalist leader, Oginga Odinga, once Jomo Kenyatta's vice president in the 1960s, and then leader of the socialist party Kenya People's Union, has been placed under house arrest and his son charged with treason. The government's anti-Luo campaign is not only a repeat of the old colonial tactic of weakening national unity by encouraging ethnic divisions, but also a disguise for the ideological campaign against the political position which Mr. Odinga symbolizes for Kenyans—radical nationalism.

President Moi, his close associate the minister for constitutional affairs, a hard-line right-winger, Charles Njonjo, and the military men such as Mulinge and Mohammed, who emerged as the strong men of the regime after the events of August 1, have a dangerously narrow domestic power base. They depend on their personal American, British and Israeli connections for military and economic support. The parallels with Latin America are inescapable: a minority, military-type, right wing, anti-intellectual government, with U.S. backing, opposes a broad cross-section of left and nationalist opinion in a spiral of violence and confrontation.

During the Kenyatta years since independence in 1963 the myth was born of a Kenya which was multiracial, liberal, tolerant—a stable haven for Western investment and for tourism. Central Nairobi, with its highrise office buildings, international chain of hotels, traffic jams, shops full of imported European goods from wine and cheese to sweaters and underwear, bookshops, cinemas and theaters offering Western low-brow entertainment, exuded prosperity and stability. An African bourgeoisie with Western tastes, a white expatriate community living in the colonial style of the 1940s, and an Asian merchant class notable for their conspicuous consumption, were the face of Kenya most visible to outsiders. It was a very partial picture born of special economic circumstances.

Kenya, in relation to other African countries, has a fairly developed capitalist economy. Colonialism provided a modern infrastructure to central Kenya, an economy based on the 4000 or so white settler farmers who, through a period of expansion in the 1930s and 1940s competed with an embryonic Asian and African capitalist class. Fast expansion of the economy went with fast Africanization at the time of independence and unusual political circumstances were produced by the fact that the minority who had the economic power were also those who had the political power.

It is rare in post-independence Africa for economic and political power to be quite so synchronized. It made, of course, for a smooth takeover from the departing British colonial power. Their proxies remained—the black, white and Asian class mentioned earlier. It was a time when economic buccaneers flourished, and new, corrupt ways of making money were devised by ingenious brains unchecked by the state, because they *were* the state. The world coffee and tea price boom, and a successful import substitution program of industrialization fed this expansionary period. Kenya became "a country of 10 millionaiares and 10 million beggars," as the MP J.M. Kariuki (one of the rare spokesmen for the poor) put it just before his assassination in 1975. The income inequities between the top 10% and the rest have become more marked each year.

And at the same time the economic realities of the invisible Kenya became gradually inescapable. A desperate land hunger worsened every year. With no ceilings on land holdings multinational companies and a handful of individuals were able to maintain vast ranches and plantations with the complicity of those in power. Kenya still has 100 farms of over 800 acres and 13 of over 40,000.

Anger over land has been boiling since independence and has erupted in many underreported incidents. In 1982, to give just a few instances, 200 squatters rioted on a 1500 acre ranch near Mombasa; a 60-man armed gang attacked guards at a pineapple farm owned by a multinational just outside Nairobi; riot police were called when a furious mob attacked the car of a rich businessman involved in a 22,000 acre co-operative settlement scheme.

And in the urban areas discontent has been equally serious. Real wages have fallen by about 10 per cent for the 1.3 million Kenyans employed in the modern urban sector of the economy. But that is becoming an ever-smaller section of urban dwellers, with a staggering 250,000 new job seekers from secondary schools and university coming onto the job market every year. Urban unemployment has been a serious problem for some years barely tackled by the government. The so-called informal sector absorbs many of these people into a twilight world of extralegal activities such as alcohol brewing, shady service industries, recycling of waste, hawking. Violence, theft, prostitution and despair are the everyday lot of those who live in the great sprawling shanty towns and squatter areas, a safe few kilometers away from the prosperous world of central Nairobi, Mombasa or the isolated tourist lodges shown to foreign visitors. On August 1 thousands of these dispossessed people surged into central Nairobi in a cathartic orgy of destruction after an early morning broadcast told them that the corrupt regime had been overthrown, political prisoners would be immediately released and Kenya returned to those who had fought for her independence.

Kenya's potentially explosive society was held together in the declining years of Kenyatta largely because Kenyans still respected his personal legitimacy as a nationalist leader in the struggle for independence from the British in the 1950s. After Kenyatta's death in 1978, and the succession of his Vice-President Daniel Arap Moi, this key to the Kenyan establishment's hold on power was lost because President Moi and his closest advisers had been on the other side in that crucial period of Kenyan history. While Kenyatta was in British detention cells in Lodwar in northern Kenya, Moi and others now in power were cooperating with the British. Moi himself was a member of the Legislative Council, Njonjo, strong man of the regime since the period of transition after Kenyatta's death, was working in the registrar's department, Jeremiah Kiereini, now chief secretary to the government, was working as a censor for the British in the Mau Mau detention camps.

The reinterpretation of the British textbook history of the 1950s to place Mau Mau in a heroic role at the center of the stage became a key strand of an ideological struggle quietly waged in Kenya in recent years mainly in the University and the cultural sphere. In 1977 the novelist Ngugi wa Thiong'o, then chairman of the literature department at Nairobi University, co-authored a play done in the Kikuyu language by the peasants of Kamiriithu Community Educational and Cultural Center on this historical theme. He was detained by Kenyatta in an attempt to crush the growing challenge from intellectual nonconformity especially among peasants. University lecturers who have done historical research on Mau Mau have been among the first targets of the government's current repression in the university. Five lecturers are now detained without trial and one imprisoned for six years for "possession of subversive literature."

The ideological nature of political struggle in Kenya has been systematically suppressed by the Western press for many years. Apart from South Africa there is nowhere on the continent which is home to nearly so many western journalists. There are more than 80 foreign journalists normally resident in Nairobi from where they travel to the rest of Africa. With a few exceptions they live in the white colonial-style ghetto and make a habit of not writing about Kenyan politics. When Kenyan politics is written about in the West it is in the misleadingly crude terms of power struggles between tribes (usually Luo versos Kikuyu); individual personalities; the economic problems supposedly caused by a high birth rate or by the arid or semi-arid nature of much of Kenya's land.

In fact such strands of politics are merely subplots in the battle between a regime whose raison d'etre is to maintain Kenya as a base for the Western capitalist concerns to which they, as individuals, are linked, and a loose coalition of nationalists who want to see a Kenya independent of foreign commercial and military interests, and where there is a check on the increasing gross inequality between the bourgeoisie and the 90 per cent of the population who are peasants and urban workers.

Since independence Kenya has been severely shaken by three political assassinations (Pio Pinto, Tom Mboya and the M.P. J.M. Kariuki), and by the detentions in 1969 of radical nationalists such as Oginga Odinga. Each upheaval has been primarily about succession, but in every crisis (except one, the assassination of Tom Mboya) the underlying issue has been the determination by the right in power to prevent debate on the fundamental political and economic choices pursued by the regime.

Kenyatta started the authoritarian trend which Moi has taken further. He muffled Parliament, turned the country's ruling party, Kenya African National Union (KANU) into a cypher, and detained those who attempted to air the issues of foreign domination in culture, the judiciary, the press and the economy, and the government's corruption and economic mismanagement. Moi has detained people for those reasons too and for challenging his move this summer to a one-party state. Through those years Kenya became more and more isolated in Africa. Her neighbor, Tanzania, whose Pan-Africanist position is widely respected in progressive Africa, has not forgiven Kenya's deliberate break-up of the East African community in 1977, or her cooperation with Idi Amin. And President Moi's year as chairman of the Organization of African Unity has served to widen the schism between left and right among African states. Within three years Moi's stewardship had brought Kenya to crisis; within just one year it had brough the OAU to near collapse. In both dramas the unseen prompter in the wings was the United States.

With the flight into exile in Tanzania in 1981 of Kenya's first political refugee, Chelagat Mutai, a radical former member of parliament, it became clear that the political temperature in Kenya was close to boiling point. The latent ideological confrontations broke the surface in February in the cultural and politcial spheres.

First, the musical *Maitu Njugira (Mother Sing for Me)* on the history of colonial Kenya acted by the same peasants from Kamiriithu Community Educational and Cultural Center and due to be performed at the National Theater in Nairobi, and to tour Zimbabwe at government invitation, was summarily suppressed by the Kenya government. The author was Ngugi wa Thiong'o who, since his release from detention with the other political detainees by Moi in late 1978, had been placed in the limbo Kenya reserves for its most articulate government critics. They become unemployable and isolated—a form of subtle torture which has broken less resilient people.

Second, in a speech timed for a week when an OAU meeting was being held in Nairobi thus guaranteeing a wide African audience for his words, Odinga strongly criticized the government for the new semisecret American base arrangements in Kenya, as well as for the record of corruption and mismanagement at the top which were daily being exposed in Nairobi papers and parliament with no action taken against the ministers said to be involved. With Mr. Odinga as he spoke was his new ally, George Anyona, a former M.P., squeezed out of politics like Odinga himself and feared by the government for his painstaking resarch into corruption and the twisting of the constitution and the judiciary. Anyona was detained by Kenyatta for his outspoken criticisms in parliament. This formidable radical alliance scared the government. And when later in the same month at a by-election in Nyeri an unknown young journalist Wangondu Kariuki got the backing for a radical election campaign from a cross-section of left-wingers from parliament, the university, and the old nationalists long out of power, the government determined to break him. He lost the election, predictably, and later in the summer was sentenced to four and a half years in prison for possession of subversive literature. Anyona and other associates of Odinga and supporters of Wangondu Kariuki have since been detained without trial. Odinga himself had his passport seized and received several tip-offs that his life was in danger. In the months before the coup attempt Kenyans increasingly spoke of an atmosphere of fear.

It is an atmosphere which has become immeasurably worse since the strange coup of August 1 which has so many unanswered questions about it.

Since August 1 the university—for a long time the target of government animosity—has been closed, and all students sent home. Before they could get away and when they reported to the administration in their home areas students were harrassed, beaten and the girls raped by the army and police. Since then numerous lecturers have been prevented from leaving the country to attend conferences or act as external examiners. Libraries have been searched for left-wing books. All oral history (which means intellectuals talking to peasants) has been banned. Lists of left-wingers have been drawn up by the government. If the university ever reopens, its spirit has been crushed as severely as was the spirit of Makerere University in Uganda under Idi Amin.

And in the subsequent police and army searches for looted goods and for those hiding Air Force personnel the level of violence against civilians has been another chilling copy of Uganda's experience. The Asian bourgeoisie who controlled so much of Kenya's economy have been traumatized and their community's slow trickle away from East Africa of the last few years looks likely to become a flood. Western private investment which has been at a near standstill for more than a year will not recover. Will U.S. government financial support, mostly on the military side, flood in to replace it? It is public knowledge that the 1980 U.S. agreement with Kenya includes facilities at Mombasa for the navy and at Nanyuki for the air force. The dredging of the harbor, extensions to the airport and new buildings will cost $50 million at Mombasa alone. The rest of the agreement is secret. Other facilities such as underground aircraft hangars have been seen at Wajir, in remote northeast Kenya, and several firms of contractors have been approached to build housing and recreation facilities on the coast which they were led to believe were intended for American residents in Kenya. Resentment of this new dependence has been widespread. Odinga's criticisms voiced in February have been applauded across the political spectrum. The Reagan administration's plans for the American Rapid Deployment Force have seriously destabilized every third world country they affect—notably Egypt and Somalia, to a lesser extent Morocco and Sudan. On other continents from South Korea and the Philippines to Chile and Central America the pattern of what happens in a Third World country swept up into this kind of American geopolitical strategic network is clear. The regime moves to the right; its alienation from the people deepens; its fear of their intellectual and cultural freedom becomes desperate; repression intensifies with the intellectual community as the primary target. Kenya today has moved a long way down this well-trodden path of American client states—intellectuals are in prison and exile, institutions of learning, books and plays are under tight government control.

But in Kenya, as in every other similar case, resistance to the regime springs up every week in new and unexpected places. The wave of writings—plays, pamphlets, books, articles—coming out of Kenya today shows the strength of cultural resistance. It has spread beyond the academic community to students, peasants, artists, Church workers, to secretaries, civil servants and the nationalist bourgeoisie. Kenya may yet prove to have been the American client most dramatically affected of them all.

---

*Victoria Brittain, writes for the London daily, *The Guardian*. In its original form the preface appeared in the November 1982 issue of *Le Monde Diplomatique*.

Introduction

A Time to Speak

A time has come when silence before the crimes of the neocolonial regime in Kenya is collusion with social evil. The government's total subservience to imperialism, its chronic economic mismanagement and blatant corruption have, with its campaign of political and cultural repression, completely isolated it from the people. Undaunted, the regime has embarked on a calculated campaign of further repression to try and smother the seeds of revolt contained in people's culture.

On March 12, 1982, the regime sent three truckloads of armed policemen to Kamiriithu Community Education and Cultural Center and razed the open air theater to the ground. Kamiriithu Open Air theater was built by the peasants and workers of the village. The day before, March 11, 1982, the regime had deregistered Kamiriithu Education and Cultural Center and banned all drama and theater activities in the area.

Three weeks earlier, the authorities had refused to allow Kamiriithu Theater Group to enter the Kenya National Theater to perform *Maitu Njugira* (Mother Sing for Me). A squad of armed policemen was at the ready to oust the group of peasants and workers should they try to force their way into the theater.

But the brutality of the philistine behavior of March 12 was a signal that the regime had embarked on a calculated campaign of cultural and political repression.

University lecturers Al Amin Mazrui, Maina-wa-Kinyatti, Edward Oyugi, Willy Mutunga, Kamoji Wachira, and Mukaru Ngang'a were arrested and later detained without trial, or sent to prison under dubious legal circumstances. Journalists such as Wangondu Kariuki were imprisoned or

1

harassed by constant police questioning. The regime later announced that it would directly control the books taught in schools and colleges. The net widened and outspoken politicians including George Anyona, were detained without trial. Khaminwa, a lawyer who took up cases of those critical of the regime, was detained without trial.

The first six months of 1982 were a watershed in the history of our country. Never before in Kenya, not even under British colonialism, has there ever been such a deliberate, carefully organized campaign of repression of ideas. What the regime really wanted of Kenyans was their unquestioning, blind loyalty to "Nyayoism," the philosophy of *follow-my-footsteps*. Questions such as, "Where are you leading us?" "Where are we going" "Follow you to do what, where, when?" were considered as seditious or even treason.

Today questioning the presence of foreign military bases and personnel (British, Israeli and U.S.) on Kenyan soil is disloyalty. Questioning colonialism is sedition. Teaching the history of the Kenyan people's resistance to colonialism is sedition. Theatrical exposure of colonial culture is sedition. Questioning the exploitation and oppression of peasants and workers is Marxism and hence treason. Questioning corruption in high places is sedition.

The pattern of repression became so clear and its aims so naked that the regime could not cover it up with sweet phrases or any pretenses of democracy.

The August 1 attempted coup came as a God-sent opportunity for the regime to root out and silence its critics. The same pattern of repression it had embarked upon has since been intensified and accelerated. More lecturers and students and critical politicians have been arrested, detained without trial or else imprisoned in the same dubious legal circumstances. More students have been killed. Many Kenyan Air Force members were killed or imprisoned even after the coup attempt was crushed. Now American and British Royal Air Force personnel fly Kenyan planes. More American and British advisers have been added to the neocolonial think-tank of the regime.

There is now an attempt to deceive the world that this widespread repression had been occasioned by the coup attempt. The extensive public relations machinery of the regime in the Western world to sell repression as new-style democracy is back in motion.

This collection of talks given in Kenya and elsewhere between 1980-1982 should go some way toward showing that, at least in the area of cultural repression, the regime had started its campaign earlier. It did not begin with August 1st! Repression of cultural expression has, in fact, been a feature of neocolonial Kenya since 1963. Under the Nyayo (following footsteps) regime, this has intensified and been codified into a program. These talks are very much in line with the positions I have taken in my writings over the years as a warning that the Kenya we have is not the Kenya that the people fought for.

The sad truth is that the neocolonial ruling regime (under Kenyatta and Moi) has arrogantly betrayed everything for which our people have struggled for because it has been able to count on the silence of us Kenyans. Thus its iron hand has been strengthened by the silence of those who have refused to speak out. Some Kenyans have preferred to moan discontent or whisper misgivings only in the sanctuary of their hearts or homes. Others have sought safety in their churches and mosques, in their workplaces or in their drinking places. Yet others are still harboring illusions that this is a democratic state even when the class in power is daily poking its dictatorial finger in their ribs and laughing sarcastically in their faces. The words of Frederick Douglass spoken in the 19th century are relevant for our Kenya today:

> The whole history of the progress of human liberty shows that all concessions, yet made to her august claims, have been born of earnest struggle. The conflict has been exciting, agitating, all absorbing, and for the time being putting all other tumults to silence. It must do this or it does nothing. If there is no struggle, there is no progress. Those who profess to favor freedom, and yet depreciate agitation, are men who want crops without plowing up the ground. They want rain without thunder and lightning. They want the ocean without the awful roar of its many waters. This struggle may be a moral one; or it may be a physical one; or it may be both moral and physical; but it must be a struggle. *Power concedes nothing without demand. It never did, and it never will. Find out just what people will submit to, and you have found out the exact amount of injustice and wrong which will be imposed upon them; and these will continue till they are resisted with either words or blows, or with both. The limits of tyrants are prescribed by the endurance of those whom they oppress.*

But Kenyans, workers, peasants, intellectuals, democrats, farmers, nationalists are waking up to their responsibilities. They have started to organize to oppose the neocolonial comprador ruling class. When Maina-wa-Kinyatti, the foremost historian of Kenyan people's anti-imperialist struggles, was sentenced to six years imprisonment, the peasants and the youths who had gathered outside the courtroom burst out with liberation songs:

> Kinyatti, the patriot, stand firm
> You are not alone
> We are all the children of the revolution
>
> It is the Unity, Unity
> Of us workers and peasants

3

Introduction

> Which will liberate Kenya from slavery.
>
> Too much fear encourages oppression
> It is better to die in the struggle
> Than to live under slavery and oppression

This book is a contribution to the continuing anti-imperialist struggle of the Kenyan people. **It is time to speak out against neo-colonial oppression.**

Freedom! Freedom! Freedom!

Hail, hail to the national patriots
Great heroes of our country.
The country and her children
Depend on your courageous leadership
Fight hard for the future of the children.

Let us unite together our compatriots
And forget tribalism and disunity
The foolish or the clever, the rich or the poor:
We should all realize
That our great aim is *Freedom!*

You, my father and my mother,
And even you my friend,
Lift your eyes and ask yourselves:
"Where is our country heading to?"

From *Thunder from the Mountains Mau Mau Patriotic Songs*
Published by Zed Press
Edited by Maina-wa-Kinyatti

Kimathi on law as a tool of oppression.

KIMATHI:

By what right dare you, a colonial judge, sit in judgment over me?
JUDGE: *[playing with his glasses, oozing infinite patience]*
Kimathi, I may remind you that we are in a court of law.
KIMATHI:
An imperialist court of law.
JUDGE:
I may remind you that you are charged with a most serious crime. It carries a death sentence.
KIMATHI:
Death . . .
JUDGE:
Yes, death . . .
KIMATHI:
To a criminal judge, in a criminal court, set up by criminal law: the law of oppression. I have no words.
JUDGE:
Perhaps you don't understand . . . . I mean . . . . we are here to deal fairly with you, to see that justice is done. Even handed justice.
KIMATHI:
I will not plead to a law in which we had no part in the making.
JUDGE:
Law is law. The rule of law is the basis of every civilized community. Justice is justice.
KIMATHI:
Whose law? Whose justice?
JUDGE:
There is only one law, one justice.
KIMATHI:
Two laws. Two justices. One law and one justice protects the man of property, the man of wealth, the foreign exploiter. Another law, another justice, silences the poor, the hungry, our people.

Kimathi on Law as a Tool of Oppression

JUDGE:

> No society can be without laws to protect property . . . I mean protect our
> lives . . . Civilization . . . Investment . . . Christianity . . . Order.

KIMATHI:

> I despise your laws and your courts. What have they done for our people?
> What?
> Protected the oppressor. Licensed the murderers of the people:
> Our people,
> whipped when they did not pick your tea leaves
> your coffee beans
> Imprisoned when they refused to "ayah"
> your babies
> and "boy" your houses and gardens
> Murdered when they didn't rickshaw
> your ladies and your gentlemen.
> I recognize only one law, one court:
> the court and the law of those who
> fight against exploitation,
> The toilers armed to say
> We demand our freedom.
> That's the eternal law of the oppressed,
> of the humiliated, of the injured, the insulted!
> Fight
> Struggle
> Change.

JUDGE:

> There's no liberty without law and order.

KIMATHI:

> There is no order and law without
> liberty.
> Chain my legs,
> Chain my hands,
> Chain my soul,
> And you cry, law and justice?
> And the law of the people bids me:
> Unchain my hands
> Unchain my legs
> Unchain my soul!

From *The Trial of Dedan Kimathi*
By Ngugi wa Thiong'o and Micere Mugo
Published by Heinemann Educational Books

Mau Mau Is Coming Back:

The Revolutionary Significance of 20th October 1952 in Kenya Today

We are here tonight for the 30th anniversary of the start of the Mau Mau war for national independence which falls on October 20th. It was on such a night in 1952 that Kenya African Union (KAU) and Mau Mau leadership were arrested. A State of Emergency was declared over Kenya by Governor Baring on behalf of the British government. Kimathi led Mau Mau Land and Freedom Army into the forests and mountains and waged an extraordinary guerrilla struggle that was eventually to compel British imperialism to seek a political solution out of the colonial impasse. Even after Kimathi's capture and subsequent execution in 1957, the Mau Mau forces never formally surrendered. It was not in fact until after independence that the Mau Mau guerrillas finally left the mountains. But what is the significance of October 20th, 1952 in Kenya today?

Why have there never been shrines erected in honor of the Mau Mau guerrilla fighters? Why has there never been a statue erected in honor of Kimathi and all those who died in the struggle for our national independence? The answers lie in the sort of independence finally settled for by Kenyatta and the Kenya African Union (KANU) leadership. Mau Mau had forced the issue but its leadership was excluded from the final settlement and done out of any power in the state. Those elements who gained out of the settlement now claim that Kenyatta (alone!) brought independence to Kenya. Kenyatta or Kimathi? KANU or Mau Mau?

The ruling regimes in Kenya have already given their own answer. They have always commemorated the date as "Kenyatta Day." But Kenyan

7

peasants and workers know it as Kimathi or Mau Mau Freedom Fighters Day. We too are celebrating October 20, 1952, as Mau Mau Freedom Fighters Day. By doing so, we are expressing solidarity with Kenyan people, for it is *their day!* The day, the month, the year Kimathi with the Kenya Land and Freedom Army started the 10-year armed struggle against imperialist colonial occupation of Kenya, to enable Kenyans to determine their economic, political and cultural life. For no people are free as long as their economy, politics and culture are controlled by imperialism!

It is therefore bitterly ironic to millions of Kenyans that as we talk here tonight, there are in Kenya three foreign military presences—the British, Israeli and American. The U.S.A. has military bases in Mombasa, Nanyuki and other places in Eastern Kenya. American and British pilots fly Kenya's airplanes. Thousands of Kenyans are in detention camps, prisons or exile. Many others have and continue to be killed. The University of Nairobi, for instance, is closed and many of our bright lecturers and students are dead or in jail or awaiting trial.

Kenyatta Day or Mau Mau Freedom Fighters Day! What's in a name? Everything, especially if it has to do with the *past*, that is with *history*. How we look at our yesterday has important bearings on how we look at today and on how we see possibilities for tomorrow. The sort of past we look back to for inspiration in our struggles affects the vision of the future we want to build. What heroes or heroines do we identify with? Waiyaki or Kinyanjui? Koitalel or Mumia? Me Katilili or Wangu Makeri? Kimathi or Kenyatta? People's leaders or colonial chiefs? Patriots or loyalists? Mau Mau fighters or Homeguards? Resistance heroes or collaborators with the imperialist enemy? Imperialist foreigners and their oppressor friends or national patriots and their comrades in struggle?

We know that when one nation conquers another nation, it tries to disfigure the history of the conquered nation. Thus when imperialist nations conquered and colonized Africa, they rewrote the history of the continent in terms of darkness preceding the European slave or colonial presence. Those who fought against the colonizing nation were depicted as villains or witches. Those who collaborated were seen in terms of outstanding courage and intelligence. In the same way and within a single nation, the dominant economic class disfigures the history of the dominated classes. Those among the dominated and exploited who took arms against those dominating and exploiting are written off as villains while those who put down people's uprisings are shown in heroic colors. Moreover, the history of that nation is often written in terms of the heroic deeds of kings, chiefs, exceptional individuals and classes, that is, in terms of those elements in that nation's past which give historical rational expression or confer legitimacy to the claims of the dominant class. The dominant class looks at history from the heights and needs of its present position.

The dominant nation or class recruits either from amongst its own or other ranks, an army of historians, philosophers, writers, journalists, in a word, intellectuals, who draw pictures of the universe corresponding to its material objective position. These become its seers, visionaries or songsters, its intellectual force. They assume the standpoint of the exploiter and oppressor. But the dominated nation or class also throws out its intellectual force either from amongst its own or other ranks which explain the world from the material basis and objective needs of the struggle of that class or nation. Such intellectuals assume the standpoint of the exploited and the oppressed.

These two intellectual forces will look at the *past* very differently, often in conflicting terms. What they have in common is an awareness of the importance of the *past* and its interpretation and they go about it with fierce commitment even when hiding under slogans of objectivity and search for truth. But it is a truth, an objectivity, from the standpoint of one or the other class. It is as if they both realize that the distance between the barrel of a gun and the point of a pen is very small: what's fought out at penpoint is often resolved at gunpoint with the possible overthrow of the one class by the other, or the overturning of the existing and apparently fixed status quo, or relations between the two contending classes or nations.

The interpretation of Kenya's past, of Mau Mau, even of the significance of October 20, 1952, is no different. Kenyatta Day or Mau Mau Freedom Fighters Day? It depends on who is looking at that crucial event and from whose viewpoint or angle of vision. Nowhere is this better illustrated than in the fierce debate that erupted among the University academic community, preceding the current repression and resistance.

II

In 1977, for instance, the editors and publishers of *The Kenya Historical Review* released a special issue on the Mau Mau Movement. The cover is a picture of British forces and their African collaborators hunting down Mau Mau Freedom Fighters in the forests of Nyandarua and Mount Kenya. Inset in the bottom right corner of the cover is a tiny frame of a pathetic face of a dead Mau Mau guerrilla made even more so by the sickly yellowish background against the luxurious green of the British forces. The editors and publishers were Kenyan. But the issue in the choice of contributions and cover illustration, and in the arrangement of the content, was clearly a scholarly attempt at the ideological burial of Mau Mau as a credible anti-imperialist nationalist movement, a kind of intellectual rationale to 80 years of Kenya's history of struggle. The triumphant tone of the introduction by Professor Ogot sounds more like an obituary of a dreaded enemy:

> We are to a large extent merely indulging in the politics of nostalgia. The Mau Mau ideology, as I have argued, was already rejected by the national-ist forces. How can we then regard Mau Mau as the pivot of Kenyan nationalism? This is a painful conclusion.

Kenyan reactionary scholarship was about to give the final coup de grace to what Kenyatta had started when in 1954 at his trial in Kapenguria; he described Mau Mau as an "evil thing" which "I have done my best to de-nounce . . . and if all other people had done as I have done Mau Mau would not be as it is now." Such scholars wearing the cloak of apparent objectivity, were burying Mau Mau in a heap of footnotes. They might well have succeeded.

But squeezed somewhere in the middle of the special issue was a well argued contribution by a brilliant and committed scholar, Maina-wa-Kinyatti, in which he took issue with the entire anti-Mau Mau intellectual establishment and described "Mau Mau as the peak of African national-ism in Kenya." He made a passionate call to Kenyan intellectuals to repudiate, in the words of Frantz Fanon, "its own nature in so far as it is bourgeois, that is to say in so far as it is the tool of capitalism, and make itself the willing slave of that revolutionary capital which is the people." He wrote:

> . . . Interest groups and individuals, including . . . some university histor-ians have started *revising* important aspects of Kenya's political history, especially of Mau Mau development. If crucial documentable occurrences of the Mau Mau movement are ignored, purposely or otherwise, if dubious new information is smuggled into the discussion, then certainly unjustifi-able analysis, deductions and conclusion will result. I insist that if our reputation is to remain worth anything or if we wish to play a positive and enlightening role in the future development of Kenya's society we must discard the speculative and encourage the objective. Clearly, a national movement that attracted hundreds of thousands of our people, a move-ment whose goals and aims were so appropriate to the common desires of so many, a movement which so profoundly influenced Kenya's political evolution and inspired so many fraternal peoples, in short, a movement which was a part of the worldwide anti-colonial onslaught cannot be dismissed merely with a flick of a pen.

Quite clearly for Maina-wa-Kinyatti, Mau Mau symbolized that revolu-tionary capital, the people, Kenyan people, third world peoples, all peoples the world over struggling against colonialist and neo-colonialist domination.

In 1980, Maina-wa-Kinyatti followed up that call for committed patriotic scholarship by editing and publishing Mau Mau songs under the title *Thunder from the Mountains—Mau Mau Patriotic Songs*. Kinyatti spent many days and nights in the homes of former Mau Mau guerrillas, peasants and workers, recording their voices as they sang, and he clearly wanted Kenyans to share with him the elation he himself had felt when listening to the guerrilla lyrics:

> One can sense the very flames of war in them. They glorify the revolutionary aspects of the movement: its dialectical relationship with the worker and peasant masses on the one hand, and its principled contradiction with British colonialism on the other. They again praise the heroism of the guerrillas and their leaders. They tell stories of outstanding battles fought by the Mau Mau forces; they speak of the patriotism of the women and youth and the great sacrifices they had to make in support of, and for participating in, the fighting. At the same time the lyrics articulate the guerrillas' deep hatred for British colonialism. They often point out that both these foreign occupiers and the local traitors should be regarded as Kenya's enemy number one who should be wiped out mercilessly. There runs through the songs a consistent spirit of optimism that the people of Kenya and their Mau Mau army will, in the end, win the war. The content of these lyrics is patriotic, anti-colonial and anti-imperialist.

But his main objective is clearly to fight against the reactionary interpretation of Mau Mau in historical scholarship. In his preface he writes:

> In summary, the main objective in translating these songs is to let them answer the anti-Mau Mau Kenyan intellectuals and their imperialist masters who, until now, continue to deny the movement's national character.

The need to answer these scholars comes from a realization that scholarship has never, and will never be neutral. Intellectuals are not disembodied voices. They stand for these or those social forces. They articulate the world outlook of this or that class. Put concretely, the question is this: if you deny Mau Mau its national character, if you, by an intellectual magic wand, were to wave it away from the central stage of Kenya's history of struggle, to whom have you left the stage? For Professor Ogot and his ilk, it is to the "nationalist forces"—rid of the deviationist Mau Mau armed struggle, of course—with which he so completely identifies: "the Mau Mau ideology was rejected by the nationalist forces. How can *we then* regard Mau Mau as a pivot of Kenya's nationalism?"

Who are Professor Ogot's *we?* Intellectuals, of course. On whose side are they? In other words, whose viewpoint, outlook, position, interests, does their interpretation of the past serve, strengthen, give historical legitimacy or scholarly expression? Clearly and unequivocally, that of the "nationalist forces" whose unexamined, unquestioned—by Ogot's intellectuals—rejection of the Mau Mau ideology in the sixties, forms the basis of these academics' logical conclusions that Mau Mau was not the pivot of Kenya nationalism. What was the Mau Mau ideology rejected by Ogot's nationalist forces? Land and Freedom. How were they to be obtained? By armed struggle. Maina-wa-Kinyatti quotes a verse from one of the Mau Mau songs:

> We shall never, never give up
> Without land on which to grow food
> And without our own true freedom
> In our country of Kenya!

Land. Freedom. A liberated Kenya. National independence. It is all there—and the uncompromising commitment—in a single verse. But in a document Kimathi published in 1953, containing seventy-nine articles, the Mau Mau ideology is further articulated:

We want an African self-government in Kenya now . . .
We reject the foreign laws in Kenya for they were not made for Kenya and are not righteous.
We reject to be called terrorists when demanding our people's rights.
Our real fight is not against the white color but is against the system carried on by the white rulers.
Fighting for our stolen land and our independence is not a crime but a revolutionary duty.
Nothing is more precious than independence and freedom. Only when we achieve our independence can our people have genuine peace.
We reject a foreign attorney general in Kenya for he deals with appearances more than righteousness.
We reject to be called Mau Mau. We are Kenya Land Freedom Army (KLFA).
We reject colonization in Kenya for being in that state we are turned into slaves and beggars.
Our people will chase the foreign exploiters, wipe out the traitors and establish an independent government of the Kenyan people . . .

The document, otherwise known as the Mau Mau Charter, was sent to the governments of India, Egypt, the Soviet Union, France, Great Britain, to the United Nations, and to pan-Africanists like George Padmore, and Kwame Nkrumah, and anticolonialists like Fenner Brockway.

Who are Professor Ogot's nationalist forces? They fall into two categories. First were the complete sell-outs, the actual *Mbwa Kalis* or watchdogs of colonialism: that is those elements who rejected the Mau Mau ideology in total and who actively fought on the side of the British colonial forces. They were the renegades otherwise known as loyalists and homeguards, active collaborators, so well described by Maina-wa-Kinyatti in his introduction to *Thunder from the Mountains:*

> Finally and most important, the songs speak out bitterly against those Kenyans, particularly the Home Guards, who betrayed the Movement to the British imperialists. In almost every song, it is made clear that the principal enemy of the Kenyan people was the British colonialists; and all those Kenyans who sided with them and helped them oppress and kill the peo-

ple were declared traitors. And war was declared on them, just as it was against the foreign occupiers. Listen to the following verses:

> You who sell us out are our great enemies
> Look around you and look at the British
> And also look at yourselves.
> The British are foreigners,
> And they will surely go back to their country
> Where will you, traitors to your country,
> Run to?

> And you traitors
> Who have joined forces with the enemy
> You will never be anything
> But the whiteman's slaves
> And when we win the war
> You will suffer for your betrayal.

Further, the songs make it very plain to the Kenyan mercenaries who were serving the British armed forces that, in helping the British to kill their compatriots, they were committing an act of treason against their nation and would be treated accordingly:

> We must continuously increase
> Our militant vigilance
> And intensify our battle
> Against these mercenaries and traitors
> Wiping them out one by one mercilessly.

In the same vein the colonial puppet chiefs were attacked:

> Don't think you are a patriot,
> When you join the enemy forces,
> Remember that to betray your people
> Is an act of treason.

In organizational terms these types were later represented by Ronald Ngala and Daniel arap Moi who led Kenya African Democratic Union (KADU) which was a black front for continued settler colonial interests. They can all be called loyalists. They concealed their sellout under nationalist slogans.

Secondly, there were those who only partially accepted some aspects of the Mau Mau ideology, those constitutionalists afraid of revolutionary change, once described by Frantz Fanon as violent in their words and reformist in their attitudes, those who, when they see the masses up in arms, rush to the colonialists to acclaim "This is very serious . . . we don't know how it will end; we must find a solution, some sort of compromise," those who use the anger of the masses as a bargaining argument for concessions and private deals with colonialism:

This idea of compromise is very important in the phenomenon of decolonization, for it is very far from being a simple one. Compromise involves the colonial system and the young nationalist bourgeoisie at one and the same time. The partisans of the colonial system discover that the masses may destroy everything. Blown-up bridges, ravaged farms, repressions and fighting harshly disrupt the economy. Compromise is equally attractive to the nationalist bourgeoisie, who since they are not clearly aware of the possible consequences of the rising storm, are genuinely afraid of being swept away by this huge hurricane and never stop saying to the settlers: "We are still capable of stopping the slaughter; the masses still have confidence in us; act quickly if you do not want to put everything in jeopardy." One step more, and the leader of the nationalist party keeps his distance with regard to that violence. He loudly proclaims that he has nothing to do with these Mau-Mau, these terrorists, these throat-slitters. At best, he shuts himself off in a no-man's-land between the terrorists and the settlers and willingly offers his services as go-between; that is to say, that as the settlers cannot discuss terms with these Mau-Mau, he himself will be quite willing to begin negotiations. Thus it is that the rear-guard of the national struggle, that very party of people who have never ceased to be on the other side in the fight, find themselves somersaulted into the van of negotiations and compromise—precisely because that party has taken very good care never to break contact with colonialism.

Organizationally, these constitutionalists eager for seats around the table to negotiate deals and pacts with colonialism, came to be represented by the Kenya African National Union (KANU) party leadership of Jomo Kenyatta and Tom Mboya. They can all be called betrayers. They concealed compromise under nationalist slogans.

It was these elements, loyalists and betrayers who received the flag from the British. Those led by Moi's KADU and Kenyatta's KANU had a common platform in their rejection of the Mau Mau ideology. It was only natural that they should merge as they did in 1964, under KANU. Hand in hand they now went on to weed out any radical elements sympathetic to Mau Mau from prominent positions in the party, government and administration. The radical nationalist leadership regrouped in the Kenya People's Union Party of Oginga Odinga and Bildad Kaggia which offered the kind of socialist alternative envisaged in the pre-independence KANU manifesto. Efforts by the Kenyatta/Mboya KANU leadership to brand KPU as just a 'tribal' affair failed. The regime then banned the Party. Over the years the Kaggias, the Oginga Odingas, the Wasonga Sijeyos, the J.M. Kariukis, the Waruru Kanjas were driven out into prisons or death. Kinyatti explains why:

After hijacking our national independence in 1963, the remnants of these traitors, with full support of the ruling compradors, began to preach "peace and brotherhood"—always invoking such slogans as "enough blood has been shed," "we all fought for independence," "Let us forget the past," etc.—in their attempt to make us forget the blood debts they owe. Since some of these individuals are now in positions of power and wealth, they have made it their main job to silence mercilessly any Kenyan patriot who speaks or writes about this heroic struggle. But if the past is any guide these efforts will be in vain. Two stanzas from the people's songs explain:

> You Home Guards must know
> We shall never forget that
> You had us put in prisons
> And treacherously revealed
> The secrets of the Africans.
>
> There can never be compromise with the traitors
> And no mercy towards them,
> For the blood of hundreds of our martyrs
> Cannot be forgotten
> And is crying for vengeance.

The Ogot-Kinyatti struggle on the interpretation of Kenya's history was thus more than an academic debate: it was an intellectual reflection of the warring, antagonistic class positions in Kenyan society since October 20, 1952. The opposed positions of Ogot's "nationalist forces" and of Mau Mau radical ideology reflect the direction Kenyan society had taken in the fifties and sixties and now in the seventies and eighties.

With the publication of *Thunder from the Mountains* two years ago and particularly Maina-wa-Kinyatti's introduction to the songs, the voice of Mau Mau began taking the offensive in the field of historical scholarship. The book was a thunderbolt in the university's academic community. Some of the people described in the book as "the leading anti-Mau Mau intellectuals" wrote to Maina-wa-Kinyatti threatening to sue him unless he apologized, withdrew the book from the market and paid for the damage to their spiritual wounds. Maina-wa-Kinyatti refused to apologize. There was expectation in the air. The interpretation of Mau Mau and our past was going to be on trial, in an open court. They hesitated. The suits never came.

Maina-wa-Kinyatti pressed on with the offensive. He collected Kimathi's papers and other original material he had gotten from his contacts with Mau Mau survivors under the title: *A Profile in Patriotic Courage: Dedan Kimathi's Letters and Documents.* At the end of 1981 he handed the completed manuscript to a publisher. In May 1982, he completed his monumental work *The History of Kenya* seen from the viewpoint of the peasantry and the working class in the tradition of Walter Rodney's *How Europe Underdeveloped Africa* and *A History of Guyanese Working Class.* In this history, the peasantry, the proletariat and the Mau Mau movement were going to occupy their rightful place in the successive struggles of Kenyan people against the Portuguese, the Arabs and the British. This was going to be the first history of Kenya written by a Kenyan. Significantly, it was to end in 1980, the formal beginning of the United States' neocolonial presence in the country with military bases in Mombasa, Nanyuki and possibly other spots in eastern Kenya. The last chapter was entitled: *The Current History of Kenya 1979-80.* At long last, Mau Mau was going to have a voice in a documented, meticulously researched and well written history by a Kenyan scholar trained in schools and universities in Kenya and America. Such a history could not be faulted on scholarship, nor could it be dismissed as wishful myth making among a poverty ridden peasantry; nor, indeed, could it be faulted on the basis that it was a work of fiction in the form of novels or theater. The news that he had been writing this history, that he had interviewed many Mau Mau cadres and generals, had for a long time been an open secret. His lectures on Kenyan, African, Black and third world history were attracting hundreds of students. The peasantry and the working class had found their voice. Mau Mau was coming back.

Maina-wa-Kinyatti had clearly angered more than just the bourgeois academic and intellectual establishment. He had frightened the men at the top whose position the academic establishment merely reflected. They who in the fifties had feared the possible consequences of the British colonialists leaving the country had invited into the country a new, more powerful neocolonial master in the United States of America. Were they perhaps disturbed by the vision of a Mau Mau coming back even though only in books and lecture halls? Could they perhaps hear in the distance the determined approach of a million awakened chanting songs similar to those of the fifties?

> You who sell us out are great enemies
> Look around you and look at the British
> And also at yourselves
> The British are foreigners
> And they will surely go back to their country
> Where will you, traitors to your country,
> Run to?

Perhaps to America!

At any rate, on June 3, 1982, Maina-wa-Kinyatti was arrested. The police raided his home in his absence. The result of four and a half months of police custody was that he had to be hospitalized in chains for an eye operation. He was then formally tried for being in possession of a "seditious" publication: *Moi's Divisive Tactics Exposed.* Among the documents produced in court as evidence of sedition and subversion was the last chapter of that monumental history: *The Current History of*

Kenya 1979-80.

The ruling authorities were trying to stage an impossible drama: they were putting Kenya history on trial for being subversive of the existing order. That order is one of repression, and exploitation of Kenyans by neocolonial forces headed by the USA and aided by proven colonial homeguards and Black Empire Loyalists. They wanted to bury that history and to silence forever those who wanted to unearth it for Kenya and the world.

So on October 18, 1982, two days before the 30th anniversary of Mau Mau Freedom Fighters Day, Maina-wa-Kinyatti was jailed for six years. Four and a half months in police custody had led to the hospital: what are six years in prison meant to do?

III

The drama was farcical, though obviously punitive and vengeful in its intention. Beneath the farce is a cruel historical irony. This: those who are presiding over Kenyan affairs—driving patriots into prisons, detentions and death—are the same people who in the fifties were actively opposing the Mau Mau struggle for independence (Moi's KADU, homeguards, and loyalists) or those that compromised the struggle for personal and family gains (Kenyatta and GEMA-type chauvinists) and made alliances with outright traitors and sellouts now grouped under the bureaucratic party skeleton labelled KANU.

I need go no further than Moi (KANU president and head of state); Charles Mugane Njonjo (Minister for Constitutional Affairs and the man who steered Kenya into a KANU ruled one-party state); Justus Ole Tipis (KANU treasurer and the minister in charge of detentions without trial); Robert Matano (KANU secretary-general); Stanley Oloitiptip (cheerleader of the Kenyatta and Moi regimes) and Jeremiah Kiereini, chief secretary and the executive head of the entire administration.

At the height of the British colonial terror campaign against Mau Mau freedom fighters and the Kenyan people, 1954-1955, Daniel Toroitich arap Moi was a colonial government appointee in the then settler run Kenya Legislative Council. He had been hand picked for the job as a good African. Later Moi, the good African, became chairman of the KADU, a Muzorewa type of black front for settler interests, whose main plank was *majimboism*, splitting an independent Kenya into regional fiefdoms. Thus up to 1963, Moi as a KADU leader was openly working against a strong united Kenya.

Charles Mugane Njonjo has a parallel record in colonial service. From 1954-60 he was an assistant registrar-general in the Registrar-General's Department. He rose to Crown Counsel, Senior Crown Counsel and Depuıy Public Prosecutor at the time of independence. Thus in 1955 and five years after, he was in active administration of the *State of Emergency Laws* that saw thousands of Kenyans hounded into prisons, detention camps and to death. His colonial service was in the family tradition. His father, Josiah Njonjo, was among the colonial chiefs to form the first ever loyalist association—that is loyal to crown and colony—in the country.

Matano, Oloitiptip and Tipis were all prominent leaders of KADU. Tipis, for instance, was its treasurer, a position he holds in today's KANU.

Jeremiah Kiereini, who has been signing the detention orders of the lecturers and others, was in the colonial rehabilitation program in detention camps. At the notorious Athi River Camp, one of his duties was to direct censorship of plays and drama sketches, making sure that only those which were anti-Mau Mau went through. He was thus the effective head of the anti-Mau Mau theater, education and culture. Indeed many of the top men in the army, police and administration in both the Kenyatta and Moi regimes were in active colonial service in the fifties.

Moi and Njonjo have at different times on different occasions singled out colonial governor Malcolm McDonald for praise for his contribution to Kenya's independence! These survivors from the colonial service, allied with Kenyatta and the elements later grouped under Gema, are, despite the often bitter struggles between them, only representatives of a social stratum, the comprador bourgeois ruling class. Absurd as it might seem or sound, this class perceives its role as effectively that of colonial restoration with themselves as the business representatives of the West and the modern landlords or white settlers in black skins. Let me illustrate:

The arrest of Maina-wa-Kinyatti on June 3, 1982, was preceded and followed by intensified cultural repression with plays being stopped and an open air theater, built by peasants and workers at Kamiriithu, razed to the gound. The plays stopped fall into three groups: those depicting the historical emergence of neocolonies as in Joe de Graft's *Muntu;* those exposing the brutality of colonial labor conditions and showing the determined struggle of the Kenyan workers against them as in *Maitu Njugira* (Mother Sing for Me); those glorifying armed resistance to colonialism as in Al Amin Mazrui's *Kilio Cha Haki* (The Cry for Justice), or those merely showing the betrayal of hopes as in *Kilio* (The Cry) by the Nairobi school students. It is quite telling that Al Amin Mazrui was himself arrested and detained without trial exactly two weeks after his play *Kilio Cha Haki* was performed at the University in May 1982.

In the same period, and in dramatic contrast to this censorship of any cultural expression that exposes colonialism was the state patronage of Western shows and procolonial culture. Thus, for instance, almost the entire establishment (ministers, civil servants, top businessmen) headed by

Charles Njonjo as guest of honor, trooped to the Kenya National Theater to see a ballet version of *Alice in Wonderland*. But even more telling was the government purchase of the television version of Elspeth Huxley's glorification of colonialism, *The Flame Trees of Thika*, which they gave prime time on national television in April and May 1982. The film is part of the current literary nostalgia for the pre-1952 settler period, not by the white settler remnants, theirs would be natural, but by top Kenyan blacks: Nairobi shops are lined with books and memoirs glorifying the colonial adventures of the early footloose aristocrats. Obviously the top men in authority identify, not with the menial servitude of the Kenyan worker or his resistance to such servitude, but with the heroic deeds of the colonial adventurers on wagon carriages, horseback or rickshaws among natives smitten dumb and wide-eyed in servile gratitude for charitable deeds and kindly light amidst the encircling gloom.

Lead kindly light: it is not an accident that the missionary—the holy race of Simpsons, Arthurs, Beechers, Carey Francises, Leakeys—is held in great esteem as the educational mentor of this class. Powerful men in to-day's Kenya virtually grovel at the feet of the missionary remnants as if still seeking approval and praise. *Father, I'll never forget that you were the first to notice me, to see that I am a good African. What I am you made me: What I have you gave me: the path you showed me, I still follow.* Well, they might show gratitude: like their colonial counterparts they have learnt the value of religion in its call for love, peace, unity and nonviolence between oppressor and the oppressed. "The colonialist bourgeoisie," wrote Franz Fanon in *The Wretched of the Earth*, "is helped in its work of calming down natives by the inevitable religion. All those saints who have turned the other cheek, who have forgiven trespasses against them, and who have been spat on and insulted without shrinking are studied and held as examples."

The Kenyan bourgeoisie is a classic case of what Fanon describes. Their leisure time when they are not attending church to count their blessings one by one is divided between collecting money from poor peasants at Harambee weekend extravaganzas; golfing and playing a little squash and tennis; relaxing in sauna baths and massage parlors; gracing shaggy dog and flower shows; visiting casinos for a little gambling and ogling at dancing nudes from abroad. Everything seems to be copied from a book, *The A.B.C. of Colonial Manners* or *Western Decorum Made Easy*. Wrote Fanon:

> In its beginnings, the national bourgeoisie of the colonial countries identifies itself with the decadence of the bourgeoisie of the West . . . [and it] will be greatly helped on its way towards decadence by the Western bour-geoisie, who come to it as tourists avid for the exotic, for big-game hunting and for casinos. The national bourgeoisie organizes centers of rest and

relaxation and pleasure resorts to meet the wishes of the Western bourgeoisie. Such activity is given the name of tourism and for the occasion will be built up as a national industry.

A caricature? Yes, but it accurately describes the infantile imitative mentality, the crass world outlook which like borrowed robes sits uneasily on them, and the total lack of any originality in the Kenya neocolonial ruling class. Their vision of society, be it economic, political or cultural, is derived from the only experience they know and care to know—the colonial economic, political and cultural order. Their image of progress, prosperity, authority, management is derived from colonialism. They have no policy directions of their own and confine themselves to carefully following the well trodden colonial paths.

Hence in industry and finance—say economically—they see themselves no more than as an attachment of the Western bourgeoisie, their mission, to quote Fanon, being "the transmission line" between the nation and imperialism. They are happy, content really, to be only the agents for international tractors, motor vehicles, pharmaceuticals, textiles, boots, canned foods and fruits, videos, television sets, bottled water, every little thing manufactured abroad. Their dormant or hidden genius glows momentarily only when devising ways of crushing any competing national initiative in all areas for which they have been paid a commission to administer. What they gloat over as being *Made in Kenya* are really branches of Western industries in the form of motor vehicle assemblies, fruit canning, textiles, papermills, shoes, tires, pins, needles, and here they are satisfied if they are made directors and receive sitting allowances or royalties for the use of their names in the company's registers or letterheads. What they call Africanization and Kenyanization was really a localization of the messenger or transmission role formerly and exclusively played by the settlers or the European representatives of the mother industries, finance houses, and big business.

But where the European representatives had the vigor—after all they really were part of the imperialist bourgeoisie—these "mimic" men have not even the blood and spirit to play their role with conviction. They are a kind of artificial limb where their European counterparts are real biological extensions of the mother capitalist class. They do not know when, where, how or what they peddle comes into being. They are like little children who blindly trust their father knows everything, and who live in the security of the "fact" that their father can right every wrong and hence have not developed the responsibility that comes with the knowledge. Their laziness, inefficiency, corruption, nepotism, ethnic chauvinism, does not make them play their messenger role efficiently. Foreign exchange reserves which should have gone into maintaining essential services have been depleted in importing expensive toys, buying houses and estates abroad, and opening secret bank accounts in Switzerland! Suddenly, as in the case of Moi's KANU regime, they wake up one morning to find that there are no more vacancies in the messenger sector—foreign investment has slowed down, increasingly unsure about the reliability of the mimic men to maintain stability—and hence their power of patronage, a little circumscribed. They become nervous. *Where is my father?* The result is the recent spectacle of Moi's New Economic Policy, unfurled with fanfare and applauded by liberal journalistic pundits and court poets. But it amounts to no more than the leader begging for European expatriates to come back and have a completely free hand in the management of our national affairs. In fact many are still there but the regime wants them to come in even bigger numbers. The export of profit will be made immeasurably easier. (But even here, there is an element of self-deception: Many companies were already carting away all the profits helped by the very greed and corruption in high places). The state will give bonuses to any company or industry that exports. Since these industries are mostly foreign owned it means taxing the already overtaxed peasantry and working class on behalf of foreign companies. Even the projects in which the state participated (after being ground to nothing by corruption and inefficiency in high places) are now up for sale to private, mostly foreign, hands at give-away prices. The new economic policy is *carte blanche* to foreign investors to do whatever they want. Even the nationalistic rhetoric with which Kenyatta used to Kenyanize the messenger role has been abandoned. Is it any wonder that even foreigners are a little wary about the new open-door policy? It is too good to be true or real. Besides, there is too much desperation in the begging tone of the leader.

In agriculture, it has been the same story. After independence, there was the rush to Africanize the inequalities of the colonial era. The state bought out the settlers. Many of the huge farms were then handed over to a few top officials in the civil service, the army and the private sector. A number of European settlers and multinationals still own huge coffee, sisal, fruit, and sugar plantations. Land hunger, the very basis of the Mau Mau struggle, haunts the vast majority of Kenyans. This situation cannot be justified by arguing that it resulted in higher productivity. On the contrary! For unlike their settler white counterparts who farmed fulltime and reinvested in "their" lands, the new owners did so on the telephone for they had fulltime jobs as government ministers, MPs, civil servants, or else were busy running after a multitude of retail and wholesale trades. Yet they wanted the state to continue guaranteeing them profits by underwriting their losses, giving them unlimited credit, and in some cases, as in the Narok wheat fields, a state agency did all the farming, harvesting and marketing and then handed over the profits to the owners. The farms handed over by the state were seen as endless sources of income and invaluable status symbols. No need to plough anything back, better bank the money abroad or buy a few transport vehicles for taxis, matatus, or goods! And trust the state or foreign expertise or more loans to come to the rescue. It was Frantz Fanon who once again prophet-ically and accurately described this phenomenon:

> The big farmers have, as soon as independence was proclaimed, demanded the nationalization of agricultural production. Through manifold scheming practices they manage to make a clean sweep of the farms formerly owned by settlers, thus reinforcing their hold on the district. But they do not try to introduce new agricultural methods, nor to farm more intensively, nor to integrate their farming systems into a genuinely national economy.
>
> In fact, the landed proprietors will insist that the state should give them a hundred times more facilities and privileges than were enjoyed by the for-eign settlers in former times. The exploitation of agricultural workers will be intensified and made legitimate. Using two or three slogans, these new col-onists will demand an enormous amount of work from the agricultural laborers, in the name of the national effort of course. There will be no modernization of agriculture, no planning for development, and no initia-tive; for initiative throws these people into a panic since it implies a minimum of risk, and completely upsets the hesitant, prudent, landed bourgeoisie, which gradually slips more and more into the lines laid down by colonialism. In the districts where this is the case, the only efforts made to better things are due to the government; it orders them, encourages them and finances them. The landed bourgeoisie refuses to take the slightest risk, and remains opposed to any venture and to any hazard. It has no intention of building upon sand; it demands solid investments and quick returns. The enormous profits which it pockets, enormous if we take into account the national revenue, are never reinvested. The money-in-the-stocking mentality is dominant in the psychology of these landed proprietors.

The result in the case of Kenya has been low farm productivity, and the burden of feeding the entire population is still on the peasantry through their individual plots or cooperatives. This means they feed others by depriving themselves. But even where the peasants have produced enough to feed the nation for a number of years as in the 1978-79 bumper corn harvest, top men in authority smuggle it to foreign coun-tries, and leave the people to starve. Once again the regime falls back on the favorite time-worn solution: begging. In 1979-80 we Kenyans saw the humiliating spectacle of the leader accompanied by nearly all his cabinet flying from one western capital to another begging for food. Begging and its corollary charity have become the central themes in an elaborate system of dependency. On this occasion the U.S. bailed them out with tons of yellow corn. The price? The regime immediately gave America military bases on Kenyan soil, our soil, without any debate or any form of consultation with parliament or with the 17 million Kenyans whose lives

would now be part of American war games! The regime, in callous disre-
gard of the wishes of the people, thus turned the country into a launching
pad for U.S. imperialist interest in Southern, Eastern and Northeastern
Africa, and the Middle East, and also placed Kenya at the frontline in the
event of a nuclear war.

Thus neither in industry nor in agriculture was there any attempt to
break with colonial structures. There was a small change though. Where
before, the country was the exclusive province of British interests, the
regime had to prove its independence and neutrality by opening the
doors of the country to wider imperialist interests from Japan, Western
Europe and the U.S. Otherwise, the comprador bourgeois elements
thought it revolutionary enough to merely insert itself in the structure by
becoming the business agents of Western capital. It is in fact erroneous to
think there is an African capitalist class in Kenya. If there was, its activities would by now have been reflected in investments in new industries, in agriculture, in manufacturing, in creative ventures, in real production, that is in the increase of use-values, real wealth. What we have had
is a class of middlemen with lucrative commissions for recycling what is
produced by peasants, or by foreign or local branches of foreign enter-
prises. Their monopoly of the state also allows them to loot the nation
through direct harambee taxation system every weekend. Here the
Kenyan regime overreaches itself: is there any other country in the world
where the President or Prime Minister or Chief of State spends every other
weekend collecting money from people on national television?

In such a situation, is it surprising that the economy is gradually grind-
ing to a halt or else marking time with less and less vigor? The foreign investors, despite the new free port policy are holding back: the lady is too
willing! As even the Grindlays Bank Group review of September 1982 put
it: "the short term outlook for the economy is not encouraging." The bank
politely describes recent agriculture production as "erratic"; manufacturing output as "well below capacity"; and high unemployment as "caus-
ing serious social problems." It continues sadly, "a steady deterioration in
the terms of trade has caused serious balance of payments difficulties. In
the past three years real personal incomes have risen marginally, if at all,"
and, the Bank concludes, "little improvement is expected in the short
term at least." The fact is that the Kenyan ruling authorities have been
able to bravely soldier on only through loans, aid and grants, from the so-
called friendly countries which means Western Europe and the U.S. The
U.S. is particularly willing because such a dependent regime gradually
turns the country into a client of the International Monetary Fund and the
World Bank and readily makes its territory and people part of the notorious U.S. Rapid Deployment Force and nuclear strategy in the Indian
Ocean. When Fanon wrote that brilliant chapter "Pitfalls of National Con-

sciousness" in *The Wretched of the Earth* he could have been writing about Kenyatta's and Moi's Kenya:

> The economic channels of the young state sink back inevitably into neo-colonialist lines. The national economy, formerly protected, is today literally controlled. The budget is balanced through loans and gifts, while every three or four months the chief ministers themselves or else their governmental delegations come to erstwhile mother countries or elsewhere, fishing for capital.

> The former colonial power increases its demands, accumulates concessions and guarantees and takes fewer and fewer pains to mask the hold it has over the national government.

The failure to break new grounds, the whole philosophy of economic *nyayoism* (which literally means the system of following the trodden paths or somebody else's footsteps), has led to mass poverty and the alienation of the regime from the people. It is this increased alienation which more immediately explains the turn the events are taking.

Over the years, the regime has responded to this alienation by becoming distrustful of the people. Compulsory public meetings are held where people are actually blamed for the poverty: women are bearing too many children. Some top government ministers are on record as saying that African women breed like rabbits! Indeed Charles Njonjo has said in parliament that parents with more than three should be penalized. "Our development plan was for 16 million people and suddenly because of irresponsibility, the population goes up to 17 million making the development plan out of date," he has told parliament. These men who do not believe in a planned economy, that is who believe that people should be at the mercy of blind free market forces, now find they can plan human beings. Any wonder that the people are scared of them? At first the regime was only alienated from ordinary peasants and workers—these poor who cannot control their appetites—but gradually the professionals like dentists, doctors, lawyers and the university community became repelled by the naked avarice of the regime. "My back is against the wall," Moi was compelled to admit in June 1982.

If you have lost faith in the people, then you cannot trust them with democracy, can you? They will spoil the game. You cannot allow them to organize anything on their own: What might they not whisper together? Thus in Kenya it is illegal for more than five people to meet without a police license. Real workers' organizations, even such bodies as University Staff Union, the Kenya Civil Servants Union and National Union of Students, are outlawed. Indeed any organization such as drama or social welfare societies which might bring ordinary people together are banned. And of course students and workers have no right to strike. There is too much democracy, Moi and his henchmen have been known to complain. So for years, opposition has been hounded into jails and detentions or harassed into an uneasy silence. Elections are few and far between and even then, popular leaders like Anyona and Oginga Odinga are barred from standing, and the results are often rigged. The party over the years became a bureaucratic skeleton manipulated into occasional motion by one or two people. In the end, this skeleton legalized itself into the only Party. Without a debate, parliament in June agreed with the President that too many parties, even if they only exist on paper, spoil the national broth. Wrote Fanon:

> In a certain number of underdeveloped countries the parliamentary game is faked from the beginning. Powerless economically, unable to bring about the existence of coherent social relations, and standing on the principle of its domination as a class, the bourgeoisie chooses the solution that seems to it the easiest, that of the single party. It does not yet have the quiet conscience and the calm that economic power and the control of the state machine alone can give. It does not create a state that reassures the ordinary citizen, but rather one that rouses his anxiety.
>
> The state, which by its strength and discretion ought to inspire confidence and disarm and lull everybody to sleep, on the contrary seeks to impose itself in spectacular fashion. It makes a display, it jostles people and bullies them, thus intimating to the citizen that he is in continual danger.The single party is the modern form of the dictatorship of the bourgeoisie, unmasked, unpainted, unscrupulous and cynical.

But in the end, the regime was even scared of the party skeleton (might it not harbor ghosts of nationalism?) and increasingly it came to rely more and more on the army and the police, thus fulfilling another of Fanon's analytical insights:

> In these poor, underdeveloped countries, where the rule is that the greatest wealth is surrounded by the greatest poverty, the army and the police constitute the pillars of the regime; an army and a police force (another rule which must not be forgotten) which are advised by foreign experts. The strength of the police force and the power of the army are proportionate to the stagnation in which the rest of the nation is sunk. By dint of yearly loans, concessions are snatched up by foreigners; scandals are numerous, ministers grow rich, their wives doll themselves up, the members of parliament feather their nests and there is not a soul down to the simple policeman or the customs officer who does not join the great procession of corruption.

You rule by fear and you are also ruled by fear. Both the Kenyatta and Moi regimes were afraid of their own army and police force. They relied instead on secret military and defense pacts with foreign powers. Kenyatta started it in 1964 with a military pact with Britain which allowed a British military presence in Kenya. Moi completed it, on a grand scale, by giving military bases to the U.S. The fact is that over the years the comprador ruling class has come to look at Kenya and its people through the eyes of a foreigner. How else explain the extreme distrust of any genuine Kenyan initiative in any area of our lives?

The identification with a foreign colonial regime is complete! The result is that what is happening in Kenya today, October 1982, is almost word for word, act for act, character for character a replay of the events of October 1952 when the British declared a State of Emergency, suspended any pretense of democracy and the rule of law, mounted cultural repression on a mass scale, killed thousands of Kenyans and hounded others to detention, prison or exile. A colonial restoration, in other words.

There is a difference, of a kind, I suppose. The theater then was colonial, the local directors being the British settler regime acting on behalf of the real masters in London. Today the theater is neocolonial, the local directors being the Kenya comprador bourgeois regime acting on behalf of the real masters in London and Washington. But there are unbroken links, economic, political, cultural and even character, between the colonial and the neocolonial theater and these are concretely illustrated in the arrest, trial and jailing of Maina-wa-Kinyatti and the detention without trial of all the other patriots.

But even more dramatic symbolism of this continuity is provided by the regime's systematic attempt at the humiliation of Oginga Odinga. He was one of the founders of KANU when it was still a nationalist party in 1960. For telling the world that Mau Mau was a heroic revolutionary struggle, Odinga was excluded from power by the British and deprived of his passport several times. Today those who were opposing KANU then are denying him any participation in the political life of Kenya by excluding him from the party he had helped found. Again he has been deprived of his passport and now he is even restricted to the town of Kisumu, under the provisions of the notorious Preservation of Public Security Act, a carry-over from the colonial state of emergency.

IV

Maina-wa-Kinyatti was ten years old when the British declared the State of Emergency all over Kenya on October 20, 1952, arrested the KAU and MAU MAU leadership, and unleashed a reign of terror which was to last for ten years. Kinyatti's father and elder brother, like thousands of other Kenyans, were imprisoned. He himself, though only a boy, was forced to go into hiding. Maina-wa-Kinyatti later, at the beginning of the sixties went to the U.S. for his undergraduate and graduate studies. The sixties in the U.S. was a period of people's awakening and Maina-wa-Kinyatti immersed himself in the Black movement and generally in the struggles of third world peoples. He was a great believer in the unity of struggles of all peoples, and particularly those of African peoples on the continent, in the Caribbean and in America. His studies and research on the history of African people, at home and abroad, had led him to see how their negative conception of themselves and their capacities was often rooted in their images of themselves acquired in the kind of historical literature they were forced to cram in schools and colleges. How people interpreted their past and their history was important in the crucial questions of where they were and where they were heading. Even the actual language used—verbs, adjectives, adverbs included—could create certain attitudes, negative or positive, toward a given event. For him people had to start with themselves, their environment and their heritage. Above all, he hated pretensiousness be it in scholarship or in life style. And of course, his sympathies with and faith in the people—ordinary workers and peasants—never wavered.

He returned to Kenya in 1973 and joined the History Department, Kenyatta University College, where his lectures and seminars started attracting a wide circle of students because in him they saw a new, fresh interpretation of history, an approach that made sense of their past and did not alienate them from Kenya. Through his efforts they were able to look at Kenya, Africa and the third world as men and women of that environment and not outsiders or foreigners. Of course he asked awkward questions: the masses were the makers of history, but how come they always lost out? What were the historical roots of the post-independence betrayal of the people? It was these questions and the fact that he put Kenya first and did not steal or buy farms or run extra businesses that have led to six years in prison. Putting Kenya first: this is what unites him with the others arrested before and after him and detained without trial.

Willy Mutunga for instance was a brilliant law lecturer in the Faculty of Law at Nairobi University. As Secretary-General of the University Staff Union (banned by Moi in 1980) he had worked tirelessly to make it into a strong organization. But perhaps his greatest crime was giving free legal advice to the poor. This was never heard of in Kenya: a lawyer giving his services free?

Kamoji Wachira, lecturer in geography, has made the only comprehensive study of Kenyan indigenous trees. He is a respected ecological consultant. What? Study Kenyan trees? Suspiciously entering forests and bushes and coming out with mere twigs and seeds? Detain this man!

Al Amin Mazrui is a brilliant linguist and writes plays in Kiswahili, about the struggles of ordinary Kenyans. He is asthmatic, has a weak heart, but works incessantly. In a society where working hard for your daily bread is despised—that's for peasants and workers!—an educated person who taxes his health draws suspicion. It is worse when such a person is taxing his health, not to amass some ill-gotten wealth, but to write in praise of the struggles of Mau Mau patriots or of peasants and workers. Why should he write a play called *The Cry for Justice* and in the language of the people?

The others are of similar breed. Edward Oyugi, expert in educational psychology, believes in and talked on the primacy of Kenyan cultures, people's cultures, in the education of Kenyans. Children can and should critically draw upon the wealth of knowledge of Kenyan people acquired in their struggles in history. He was also a trustee of the University Staff Union. Mukaru Ng'ang'a, a historian, did research among ordinary peasants and chose to spend his time in the villages and write about the Mau Mau struggles.

The two politicians, George Anyona and Koigi-wa-Wamwere, both detained by Kenyatta and now by Moi, were conspicuous, not only as consistent critics of corruption and who never amassed wealth, but also for their hard work and attention to detail. As for Khaminwa, lawyer and advocate of the High court, he had the audacity to be faithful to his professional ethic and take up the cases of even those at loggerheads with the president—Anyona and Odinga for instance.

I could go on!

The fact is that at the University of Nairobi and Kenyatta College there had, over the years, developed a new breed of young scholars—bright, confident, original, honest—whose simple life style was a stunning contrast to the dominant imported culture of borrowed plumes. They fit the Fanonist honest, anti-imperialist intellectual:

> In underdeveloped countries, there are certain members of the elite, intellectuals and civil servants, who are sincere, who feel the necessity for a planned economy, the outlawing of profiteers and the strict prohibition of attempts at mystification. In addition such men fight in a certain measure for the mass participation of the people in the ordering of public affairs.

In the mentality of the Kenyan ruling class, to put Kenya first; to love Kenya; to have faith in the capacity of the people to change their lives; to insist that people are the subjects and not just the passive objects of development; to insist on certain minimum professional ethics and democratic principles; to reveal that ordinary peasants and workers struggled for liberation; to sing praises to the Mau Mau movement; to write positively about the anti-imperialist heroes of Kenyan history—Me Katilili, Koitalel, Waiyaki, Nyanjiru, Kimathi; to reject foreign bases; to reject a society based on corruption; to reject the rule of fear; to oppose imperilism and its local Kenyan allies, is *a crime*. Above all, to criticize the slave philosophy of nyayoism—that is the mentality of always following in the footsteps of the U.S. and Britain; the policy of begging and charity; the program of looting the peasantry and working class; the chronic dependence complex—is sedition, subversion and treason.

For such crimes many Kenyans—lecturers, lawyers, writers, journalists, students, democrats, peasants and workers—have been incarcerated in the very prisons and detention camps originally built by the

British colonial settler regime to hold Mau Mau Freedom Fighters and other patriots. Maina-wa-Kinyatti for instance was in the very prison cells where his father and elder brother were held during the colonial State of Emergency declared over Kenya on October 20, 1952!

V

What then is the significance of October 20, 1952 in Kenya today? The date brought suffering to us Kenyans, on a scale hitherto unknown. People's newspapers and books were banned. Writers and journalists were jailed for sedition. People's cultural organizations were banned. People's schools were outlawed, others literally razed to the ground. Our people's culture was being strangled: patriotic songs and dances for instance meant prison for the composers and singers. Workers' organizations were banned and their leaders jailed. Strikes were banned. Political parties were banned. Ban this, ban that, ban, ban, burn. The British Army and administration killed our men, women and children. They hounded thousands of others into prisons and detention camps. The rest of the population was incarcerated in "protected" villages where many more died of starvation and beating by the British-led homeguards. Our women were raped. Men and women were tortured in the most brutal revolting fashion. Death, detention, prison, and exile: October 20, 1952, was the start of a 10-year rule of colonial terror.

But the same years saw the Kenyan people organize and resist on a scale they had never before attempted. People, peasants and workers, organized in their villages, towns, fields, forests, mountains and refused to be cowed by the colonial tyrant. Led by the Mau Mau, they fought back, deliberately, consciously, tenaciously, courageously, driven on and strengthened by their conviction that their anticolonial cause was right and just. In short, the extreme and well organized repression of the British-imposed State of Emergency called forth in Kenyan people organized resistance on a scale that later forced British colonialism to concede independence. Organized repressive terror was met by organized revolutionary resistance! Had not that been the lesson they had learnt from their history?

When British colonialism invaded Kenya at the turn of the century, they were resisted by the different nationalities in Kenya. Waiyaki, Koitalel, Me Katilili: they all led people's armies against the colonial occupiers. But they were defeated by the superior British weaponry, the superior British organization, and also, we must admit, by internal divisions within each nationality and between the different nationalities. As a result our land was taken away and for the first time in our history there was born a wage-earning class. Capitalism had entered Kenya: we were now connected to the world system of imperialism in the colonial stage. So our land, our labor, and our wealth were taken from us. Forced labor, taxation, slave conditions became our lot. We had no control over our lives. But once again our people regrouped, they rejected ethnic divisions and in the twenties, thirties and forties, they once again organized against British colonialism. The working class born in the new coffee, tea, sisal, sugar cane and wheat plantations, the agricultural proletariat, and its counterpart in towns, born of the new commerce and industry, the industrial proletariat, though small in number, led the peasantry to wage a national cultural and political resistance. In 1922 workers of all nationalities marched to the Central Police Lines in Nairobi to demand the release of Harry Thuku, the workers' leader. They were led by Mary Nyanjiru. She and 150 others were shot dead.

Meanwhile a cultural movement swept through the land. The Muthirigu dancers and poets; the Mumboist singers; even the Dini-ya-Mswambwa artistes—these were cultural manifestations of an anticolonial resistance. These struggles found political expression in the anticolonial nationalist organizations, which, although based in different nationalities, were united by the anti-imperialist content of their demands and assertions. Once again the nationalist leaders were jailed, detained or exiled. People's cultural and political organizations were banned. Defeat? No. For in the fifties they came back and organized at a higher level to deal a mortal blow to British colonialism not only in Kenya but in Africa. The Mau Mau armed struggle was the first of its kind in Africa: Others FLN, MPLA, FRELIMO, ZANLA, etc. were to come later.

That is the main lesson of Kenya history. People's movements were suppressed, sometimes even weakened by religious and ethnic divisions deliberately sown among them, but they would re-emerge at a higher level, stronger, brighter, more determined. People's leaders were imprisoned. But others emerged and quietly took up the baton of struggle. In Kenya, autocracy has always met with popular opposition, repression with resistance, reactionary violence with revolutionary heroism.

That spirit of resistance in Kenyan history is today being exemplified by the astonishing composure of the young students who, without lawyers, and in court on sedition charges which bring 10 years in jail, courageously call for power to the people even as they are led away in chains.

After Maina-wa-Kinyatti was sentenced to six years in prison, the crowd of peasants and workers, some of whom had come from more than 50 miles away, burst into defiant liberation songs. Police charged into them but according to the *Daily Nation* of October 19, 1982, "the police had a hard time dispersing the crowd of women from the court corridors." The lesson of that gesture, two days before October 20, the 30th anniversary of the Mau Mau armed struggle, was not lost on Kenyans. As the *Guardian* of October 19, 1982 commented:

> The trial and its verdict are clearly intended as a government warning to Kenyans of the consequences of dissent. But the highly unusual singing demonstrations outside the courtroom, mostly by middle-aged country women, is an indication that the Mau Mau ideals that Kinyatti symbolizes for many ordinary Kenyans are still strong 30 years later.

What are these ideals so shamelessly betrayed? Land, food, houses, jobs, education, unity of Kenyan people, democracy, independence. But more than this. For in the words of Fanon,

> Independence is not a word which can be used as an exorcism, but an indispensable condition for the existence of men and women who are truly liberated, in other words who are truly masters of the material means which make possible the radical transformation of society.

That for me is the revolutionary significance of October 20, 1952, in Kenya today: repression by the powerful met by the indomitable resistance of those they thought powerless to liberate Kenya from neocolonialism, what Oginga Odinga once described as a state of Not Yet Uhuru. And as Mau Mau was a precursor of armed liberation armies against colonialism in Africa, so is today's struggle in Kenya against a neocolonialism now led by the U.S. part of the worldwide people's battle against imperialism. The spirit of Mau Mau is coming back!

London
October 22, 1982

---

*This paper was written for the 30th Anniversary of the Mau Mau Freedom Fighters Day. It was delivered in London on October 22, 1982 at a meeting organized by the Committee for the Release of Political Prisoners in Kenya.

Declaration of War in Kenya

When the war was declared in 1952
Our country was turned into a huge prison.
Innocent people, men, women and children,
Were herded into concentration camps,
Under all kinds of harsh repression.

Kenyan patriots were arrested and killed,
Thousands of others were subjected
To slow death in Manyani
And Mackinnon Road concentration camps.

Large-scale massacres of our people
Were committed across the country.
Meanwhile Kimathi in Nyandarwa called for total mobilization,
He told the people to unite and fight
These foreign murderers with heroism
And drive them out of the country.

Our Independent Schools, the people's schools,
Were turned into gallows
Where many of our compatriots
Experienced untold suffering and death.

Our livestock were confiscated
And our crops in the fields were destroyed.
All public markets were closed down
And all people's newspapers were banned.

Later the colonialists employed
Vast numbers of Kenyans who took up rifles
To fight as mercenaries in opposition to the Motherland,
To kill and torture their own compatriots
Leaving behind countless widows and orphans.

In spite of harsh enemy repression,
The revolutionary flame was maintained and developed.
And people's hatred toward the British oppressors
Grew from day by day,
And proudly they declared:
'It would be better to die on our feet
Than to live on our knees.'

From *Thunder From the Mountains*

A Worker Talks to a Peasant

GICAAMBA:
   Look at me.
   It's Sunday.
   I'm on my way to the factory.
   This company has become my God.
   That's how we live.
   You wake up before dawn.
   You rub your face with a bit of water
   Just to remove dirt from the eyes!
   Before you have drunk a cup of milkless tea,
   The Siren cries out.
   You dash out.
   Another siren.
   You jump to the machine.
   You sweat and sweat and sweat.
   Another siren.
   It's lunch break.
   You find a corner with your plain grains of maize.
   But before you have had two mouthfuls,
   Another siren,
   The lunch break is over.
   Go back to the machine.
   You sweat and sweat and sweat.
   Siren.
   It's six o'clock, time to go home.
   Day in, day out,
   Week after week!
   A fortnight is over.
   During that period
   You have made shoes worth millions.
   You are given a mere two hundred shillings,
   The rest is sent to Europe.
   Another fortnight.
   You are on night shift.
   You leave your wife's sweat.
   Now you are back at the machine.
   You sweat and sweat and sweat,
   You sweat the whole night.
   In the morning you go home.
   You are drunk with sleep.
   Your wife has already gone to the fields.
   You look for the food.
   Before you have swallowed two mouthfuls,
   You are dead asleep.
   You snore and snore.
   Evening is here!

A Worker Talks to a Peasant

You meet your wife returning from the fields.
Bye, bye,
You tell her as you run to the machine.
Sweat.
Another fortnight.
Here, take this
Two hundred shillings.
The rest to Europe.
By that time you have sold away
Your body,
Your blood,
Your wife,
Even your children!
Why, because you hardly ever see them!
There are some who sell away their blood,
And they end up dying in there.
But many more end up as cripples.
Remember the son of . . . eeeh . . . you know who I mean . . .
The chemical dust
Accumulated in his body
Until the head cracked!
Did they take him to hospital?
Oh, no.
Was he given any compensation?
He was summarily dismissed, instead.
What about the son of . . . eeh . . .
You know the K.C.A.* elder? The one
Who, with others, started the freedom struggle? . . .
His son used to work in the cementing section
Where they keep retex and other dangerous chemicals.
The chemicals and the dust accumulated in his body,
He was forced to go to the Aga Khan Hospital for an operation.
What did they find inside him? A stone.
But was it a stone or a mountain!
It was a mountain made of those chemicals!
He was summarily retired with twenty-five cents as compensation.
What has life now got to offer him?
Is he not already in his grave though still breathing?
Since I was employed in that factory,
Twenty-one people in that section have died.
Yes, twenty-one people!
KIGUUNDA:
Oooh, this is a very serious matter!
If I were to be told to work in that retex section
I, son of Gathoni,
Would then and there part ways with that company.

---
*K.C.A.: Kikuyu Central Association, a militant political movement.

34

GICAAMBA:

I wouldn't mind, son of Gathoni,
If after selling away our labor,
Our village had benefited.
But look now at this village!
When was this company established?
Before the Second World War.
What did it bring into the country?
A few machines,
And money for erecting buildings to house the machines.
Where did they get the land on which to build?
Here!
Was it not this factory together with the railways
Which swallowed up all the forests around?
Is that not why today we cannot get firewood
And we can't get rain?
Where do they get the animal skins?
Here!
Where do they get the workers to work those machines?
Here!
Where do they get the buyers for those shoes
Here!
The little amount of money they give us.
We give back to them;
The profit on our work,
On our blood,
They take to Europe,
To develop their own countries.
The money they have already sent to Europe
Paid for those machines and buildings a long time ago.
Son of Gathoni, what did I tell you?
A handful of peanuts is thrown to a monkey
When the baby it is holding is about to be stolen!
If all the wealth we create with our hands
Remained in the country,
What would we not have in our village?
Good public schools,
Good houses for the workers,
Good houses for the peasants,
And several other industries
In which the unemployed could be absorbed.
Do you, son of Gathoni, call this a house?
And remember the majority are those
Who are like me and you!
We are without clothes.
We are without shelter.
The power of our hands goes to feed three people:

A Worker Talks to a Peasant

Imperialists from Europe,
Imperialists from America,
Imperialists from Japan,
And of course their local watchmen.
But son of Gathoni think hard
So that you may see the truth of the saying
That a fool's walking stick supports the clever:
Without workers,
There is no property, there is no wealth.
The labor of our hands is the real wealth of the country.
The blood of the worker
Led by his skill and experience and knowledge
Is the true creator of the wealth of nations.
What does that power, that blood, that skill
Get fortnight after fortnight?
Something for the belly!
Wa Gathoni, just for the belly!
It's just to bribe the belly into temporary silence!
What about the three whom I mentioned?
Today all the good schools belong
To the children of the rich.
All the big jobs are reserved
For the children of the rich.
Big shops,
Big farms,
Coffee plantations,
Tea plantations,
Wheat fields and ranches,
All belong to the rich.
All the good tarmac roads lead to the homes of the rich.
Good hospitals belong to them,
So that when they get heart attacks and belly ulcers
Their wives can rush them to the hospitals
In Mercedes Benzes.
The rich! The rich!
And we the poor
Have only dispensaries at Tigoni or Kiambu.
Sometimes, these dispensaries have no drugs,
Sometimes people die on the way,
Or in the queues that last from dawn to dusk . . .
WANEGECI:
Oh, well, independence did come!
NJOOKI: *(Sings Gitiiro*)*
Let me tell you
For nobody is born wise

---

*Gitiiro: name of a dance song, a form of opera.

So although it has been said that
The antelope hates less he who sees it
Than he who shouts its presence,
I'll sing this once,
For even a loved one can be discussed.
I'll sing this once:
When we fought for freedom
I'd thought that we the poor would milk grade cows.
In the past I used to eat wild spinach.
Today I am eating the same.

GICAAMBA: *(Continuing as if he does not want his thoughts to wander away from the subject of foreign-owned companies and industries)*

Yes,
What did this factory bring to our village?
Twenty-five cents a fortnight.
And the profits, to Europe!
What else?
An open drainage that pollutes the air in the whole country!
An open drainage that brings diseases unknown before!
We end up with the foul smell and the diseases
While the foreigners and the local bosses of the company
Live in palaces on green hills, with wide tree-lined avenues,
Where they'll never get a whiff of the smell
Or contract any of the diseases!

KIGUUNDA: *(Sighs and shakes his head in disbelief)*

Oooh!
I have never worked in a factory.
I didn't know that conditions in industries are that bad.

GICAAMBA:

To have factories and even big industries
Is good, very good!
It's a means of developing the country.
The question is this: Who owns the industries?
Who benefits from the industries?
Whose children gain from the industries?
Remember also that it's not only the industrial tycoons
Who are like that!
Have you ever seen any tycoon sweating?
Except because of overweight?
All the rich wherever they are . . .
Tajiri wote duniani . . .
Are the same,
One clan!
Their mission in life is exploitation!
Look at yourself.
Look at the women farm laborers,
Or those that pick tea-leaves in the plantations:

A Worker Talks to a Peasant

How much do they get?
Five or seven shillings a day.
What is the price of a kilo of sugar?
Five shillings!
So with their five shillings:
Are they to buy sugar,
Or vegetables,
Or what?
Or have these women got no mouths and bellies?
Take again the five shillings:
Are they for school fees,
Or what?
Or don't those women have children
Who would like to go to school?
Well, independence did indeed come!

From *I Will Marry When I Want*
by Ngugi wa Thiong'o and Ngugi wa Mirii
Published by Heinemann Educational Books

Women in Cultural Work:

The fate of Kamiriithu
people's theater in Kenya

In the Gikuyu language play *Ngaahika Ndeenda* which has now come out in English as *I will marry when I want,* a factory worker finds a peasant mother weeping over, among other things, the fact that her daughter is now employed as a barmaid, one of the most insecure, low paid and humiliating jobs in Kenya and into which hundreds of girls are forced in the modern Kenya dancing to the tune of U.S. military bases, the International Monetary Fund and the World Bank. Working in a bar is, to the peasant, the same as becoming a whore:

GICAAMBA: *[Moving away from the board]*
    Let's not call our children prostitutes.
    A hyena is very greedy
    But she does not eat her young.
    Our children are not to blame.
    Gathoni is not to blame.
    When a bird in flight gets very tired
    It lands on the nearest tree.
    We the parents have not put much effort
    In the education of our girls.
    Even before colonialism,
    We oppressed women
    Giving ourselves numerous justifications:

Women in Cultural Work

[Sings]

> *Women and property are not friends,*
> *Two women are two pots of poison,*
> *Women and the heavens are unpredictable,*
> *Women cannot keep secrets,*
> *A woman's word is believed only after the event.*

And through many other similar sayings,
Forgetting that a home belongs to man and woman,
That the country belongs to boys and girls.
Do you think it was only the men
Who fought for Kenya's independence?
How many women died in the forests?
Today when we face problems
We take it out on our wives,
Instead of holding a dialogue
To find ways and means of removing darkness from the land.

[Sings]

> *Come my friend*
> *Come my friend*
> *Let's reason together.*
> *Our hearts are heavy*
> *Over the future of our children.*
> *Let's find ways of driving darkness*
> *From the land.*

NJOOKI:
    Gathoni now has no job.
    She has no other means of earning a living
    And she would like to dress up
    Like all her age-mates.
WANGECI:
    Would she were a housemaid!
NJOOKI:
    A housemaid!
    To be collecting all the shit in somebody else's house?
    And when the memsahib is out of sight,
    The husband wants the maid to act the wife!
    Thus the maid doing all the work for memsahib!
GICAAMBA ⎫   *[Sing as if continuing the song*
NJOOKI   ⎬   *Gicaamba has just sung.]*
Yes we find out why
It's the children of the poor
Who look after rich people's homes,
Who serve them beer in beer-halls,
Who sell them their flesh.

Come my friend
Come my friend
We reason together.
Our hearts are heavy
Over the future of our children.
Let's find ways of driving away darkness
From the land.

WANGECI:

Oh, my child!

NJOOKI:

She will come back!
Our children will one day come back!

The passage shows the double oppression of women. As suppliers of labor in colonies and neocolonies, they are exploited; and as women they suffer under the weight of male prejudices in both feudalism and imperialism.

But the passage shows two other things: the need to look for causes and solutions in the social system of how wealth is produced, controlled and shared. This calls for the unity of the workers and peasants—without sexist prejudices—against imperialism and all its class allies in the colonies and neocolonies.

In the specific case of Kenya, the passage pays tribute to the important role women have always played in our history. They have been at the forefront in all its crucial and decisive phases.

The wars against the British colonial occupation of Kenya, for instance, threw to the fore the leadership of Me Katilili. She was in her seventies when she organized the Giriama youth in the 1913-14 armed struggle against the British colonial administration. She was arrested and detained but she never gave in to her torturers.

The 1920s also saw a great awakening among workers of all nationalities and they united in a great workers movement demanding an end to forced labor, the carrying of identity papers, taxation, slave wages and all other oppressive features of the colonial system like the beating of workers and the prostitution of teenage girls by the settler plantation owners. The British retaliated by arresting and detaining Harry Thuku, the leader of the workers' movement. The biggest demonstration of workers then ever seen in Kenya demanding his release was led by Mary Muthoni Nyanjiru. She was among the first to be shot dead by the British forces followed by 150 others in what has now come to be known as the 1922 massacre.

The 1950s saw the Mau Mau armed struggle and Kenyan women played a heroic role in the fighting in the forests and mountains, and in prisons and detention camps, and in the homes. They were everywhere.

This is the kind of history and struggle that the play *Ngaahika Ndeenda (I will marry when I want)* was celebrating.

The play was performed by members of Kamiriithu Community Education and Cultural Center, Limuru, Kenya, in 1977. Over two thirds of the members were women ranging from children to those in their seventies. They were mostly poor peasants, plantation workers, the unemployed school dropouts, and one office secretary. Together with the men—factory workers, poor peasants, the unemployed, primary school teachers, and university lecturers—they had built an open air theater with a seating capacity of over 2000. Although the script was drafted by Ngugi wa Mirii and I, the peasants and workers added to it, making the end product a far cry from the original draft. Everything was collective, open and public, and it was fascinating to see a unity gradually emerge virtually rubbing out distinctions of age, education, sex and nationality. The evolution of this community center is described in my book *Detained: A Writer's Prison Diary,* and I cannot find better words with which to describe the transformation I experienced and saw with my own eyes:

> The six months between June and November 1977 were the most exciting in my life and the true beginning of my education. I learnt my language anew. I rediscovered the creative nature and power of collective work.
>
> Work, oh yes, work! Work, from each according to his ability for a collective vision, was the great democratic equalizer. Not money, not book education, but work. Not three-piece suits with carnations and gloves, not tongues of honey, but work. Not birth, not palaces, but work. Not globetrotting, not the knowledge of foreign tongues and foreign lands, not dinners at foreign inns of court, but work. Not religions, not good intentions, but work. Work and yet more work, with collective democratic decisions on the basis of frank criticisms and self-criticism, was the organizing principle which gradually emerged to become the corner-stone of our activities.
>
> Although the overall direction of the play was under Kimani Gecau, the whole project became a collective community effort with peasants and workers seizing more and more initiative in revising and adding to the script, in directing dance movements on the stage, and in the general organization.
>
> I saw with my own eyes an incredible discipline emerge in keeping time and in cutting down negative social practices. Drinking alcohol, for instance. It was the women's group, led by Gaceeri wa Waigaanjo, who imposed on themselves a ban on drinking alcohol, even a glass, when coming to work at the center. This spread to all the other groups including the audience. By the time we came to perform, it was generally understood and accepted that drunkenness was not allowed at the center. For a village which was known for drunken brawls, it was a remarkable achievement of our collective self-discipline that we never had a single incident of fighting or a single drunken disruption for all the six months of public rehearsals

and performances.

I saw with my own eyes peasants, some of whom had never once been inside a theater in their lives, design and construct an open-air theater complete with a raised stage, roofed dressing-rooms and stores, and an auditorium with a seating capacity of more than two thousand persons. Under a production team led by Gatoonye wa Mugoiyo, an office messenger, they experimented with matchsticks on the ground before building a small working model on which they based the final complex.

The rehearsals, arranged to fit in with the working rhythms of the village, which meant mostly Saturday and Sunday afternoons, were held in the open, attracting an ever-increasing crowd of spectators and an equally great volume of running appreciative or critical commentaries. The whole process of play-acting and production had been demystified and the actors and the show were the gainers for it. The dress rehearsal on Sunday, September 25, 1977, attracted one of the biggest crowds I have ever seen for a similar occasion, and the same level of high attendance was maintained for the next four Saturdays and six Sundays.

Furthermore, the whole effort unleashed a torrent of talents hitherto unsuspected even by the owners. Thus before the play was over, we had already received three scripts of plays in the Gikuyu language, two written by a worker, and one by a primary school teacher. One unemployed youth, who had tried to commit suicide four times because he thought his life was useless, now suddenly discovered that he had a tremendous voice which,when raised in a song, kept its listeners on dramatic tenter-hooks. None of the actors had ever been on a stage before, yet they kept the audiences glued to their seats, even when it was raining. One of the most insulting compliments came from a critic who wrote that the orchestra was professional and had been hired from Nairobi. Another insulting compliment came from those who heatedly argued that simple villagers could never attain that excellence; that the actors were all university students dressed in the tattered clothes of peasants. Another equally insulting compliment came from a university lecturer in literature who argued that the apparent effortless ease of the acting was spontaneous: after all, the villagers were acting themselves. The fact was that all the actors and musicians, men, women and children, came from the village, and they put in more than four months of conscious disciplined work. Some of our university lecturers and those other critics, in their petty-bourgeois blindness, could never conceive peasants as being capable of sustained disciplined intellectual efforts.

For myself, I learnt a lot. I had been delegated to the role of a messenger and porter, running errands here and there. But I also had time to observe things. I saw how the people had appropriated the text, improving on the language and episodes and metaphors, so that the play which was finally put on to a fee-paying audience on Sunday, October 2, 1977, was a far cry from the tentative awkward efforts originally put together by Ngugi and myself. I felt one with the people. I shared in their rediscovery of their collective strength and abilities, and in their joyous feeling that they could accomplish anything—even transform the whole village and their lives without a single Harambee of charity—and I could feel the way the actors were communicating their joyous sense of a new power to their audience who too went home with gladdened hearts.

Before long the center received delegations from other peasant communities who wanted similar cultural ventures in their areas. A peasant/worker theater movement was about to start.

But unfortunately the Kenyan government struck with vengeance. The public performances of the play were stopped on November 16, 1977, and I was later arrested.

For the next three years or so, there were no theater activities in the center. Adult literary classes continued, and once again women were the main participants.

Then in November 1981, the group reassembled ready to tackle yet another play. This time it was a musical, *Maitu Njugira (Mother Sing for Me)*, set in the 20s and 30s when Kenyan workers were struggling against repressive labor conditions. The Kamiriithu group was ready to put on the show at the Kenya National Theater on February 19, 1982, but the Kenyan authorities refused the group permission to publicly perform the play. In Kenya, a drama group has to be registered: even then such a group has to get a license for each play they want to perform. The group retaliated by continuing with rehearsals at Nairobi University but making them public. The rehearsals went on for seven days during which at least 10,000 people were able to see the show. The government finally stopped the rehearsals.

The fate of the Kamiriithu Theater is described in a statement I was asked to make on March 10, 1982. To understand the frustrations which a progressive rural and community based theater movement faces in neocolonial Kenya, I reproduce the statement.

But there is another reason for reproducing it. Lately and in response to widespread national and international criticism of the Kenya government's willful destruction of Kamiriithu Theater, the President of the Republic, H.E. Daniel Arap Moi, has been making public speeches saying that Kamiriithu was teaching politics under the cover of culture. Our statement is a detailed documented account of the group's tireless efforts in vain to get a response from the government and it shows the total contempt the regime for his people's efforts. The statement was released to both the Kenyan and international press at a conference in Nairobi.

...I have been asked by the management committee of Kamiriithu Theater Group and those responsible for the production of our new play, *Maitu Njugira*, to express the following observations regarding our efforts to obtain a government stage license for the Kenya National Theater.

First I must express our extreme disappointment and even much anger at the grossly irresponsible manner which the authorities concerned chose to deal with our application for the license, normally a quick routine administrative procedure, unnecessary in most countries, but introduced in most British colonies as a method of vetting and censoring native cultural expression.

Dutifully we applied for this license in writing on November 2, 1981, to the Nairobi Provincial Commissioner. We then followed up this with a reminder on November 12, 1981. On November 18, 1981 we got a letter from the Nairobi Provincial Commissioner's Office asking us to do something that no other theater group has ever been asked to do, that is, to go back to the District Commissioner, Kiambu, to ask for a recommendation, this on the pretext that the physical address of our Group was in Kiambu. Still we went ahead and on November 23, 1981, we wrote to the District Commissioner, Kiambu, asking for a recommendation. We have never received a reply from Kiambu but throughout December 1981 and January 1982 the chairman of our group, Mr. Ngugi wa Mirii, kept running between Kiambu and Nairobi trying to get a reply and the result of our application. On February 3, 1982, we wrote a second reminder to the Nairobi Provincial Commissioner. On February 16, 1982, three days before the scheduled opening of our performances at the Kenya National Theater, we wrote a third reminder, which we even copied to the Chief Secretary.

To all these letters and reminders, the Government, through the Nairobi Provincial Commissioner, never responded in writing. Instead the management of the Kenya National Theater were given secret instructions not to allow our group into the theater either for the technical rehearsals starting on February 15 or for the opening night of February 19. The police must have also been given instructions to harass us, for on February 19 the police kept patrolling the grounds of the Kenya National Theater where our Group sat singing, waiting for a last minute reply to our application for the stage license.

After February 19, our group resumed rehearsals at the Theater Two of the University of Nairobi where we had been rehearsing. But once again on February 25, the university authorities were instructed by telephone not to allow us the use of their premises. I would like to make it clear that up to now the government has not formally written to us about the fate of our application.

By so doing, the government denied us one of the most elementary human and democratic rights: the right of every human community to cultural expression. The administration's handling of the matter showed total insensitivity to the sheer amount of labor, effort and money put up by a village group over a three months' period. By refusing us a license, the administration denied Kenyans the right to an entertainment of their choice. The fact that the rehearsals attracted over 10,000 people was an indication that they wanted the show. The play which heavily drew from the songs and dances of different Kenyan nationalities showed practical possibilities for the integration of Kenyan cultures. And as brilliantly directed by Waigwa Wachira and Kimani Gecau, the play suggested a whole new basis for Kenyan theater. It now looks as if Kenyans, especially peasants, are not supposed to dance, sing and act out their history of struggle against colonial oppression.

The play *Maitu Njugira* draft written by myself and subsequently enriched by the cast is what may be called a dramatized documentary on the forced labor and "Kipande" laws in the colonial Kenya of the twenties and thirties. It shows the attempts in one community to repulse these and other injustices and to survive as a unit despite tremendous official intrigue and brutality. It shows indirectly the genesis of some of our peoples' subsequent political movement and the seeds of their defeats and partial triumphs.

This play is unlike our earlier effort at communal drama, *Ngaahika Ndeenda*, whose staging was stopped without explanation by the government in 1977 after a highly acclaimed brief run and whose basic theme revolved around present day Kenyan society. Understandably, the wealthy who control the government did not like the stark realities of their own social origins enacted on the stage by simple villagers. As a result, we were harassed, even some of us detained as you know. We did not apologize. We still believe in and stand by the content of that play. The spirit of the Center (that is, Kamiriithu Community Educational and Cultural Center) was not killed or even impaired.

Maitu Njugira by contrast addresses itself to the rulers of a previous, albeit related, era and it came to us as curious that the ghosts of the settler colonial regime of the thirties should in 1982 come to haunt the same tiny circle of wealth that *Ngaahika Ndeenda* so terrified. It now seems, despite constitutional safeguards, that any public examination of Kenya's society, its history or future cannot be done without raising the nervousness of the authorities.

We consider this attitude undemocratic and extremely dangerous. It is our right to represent our art and culture from our own viewpoint so long as in the process no extant law is broken. We have sought to act strictly according to law and with complete legitimacy in all aspects of our work. We have followed the unnecessarily difficult and frustrating due process of registering ourselves, applying for permits and all the other now commonplace prerequisites of self-expression in Kenya. We have been very patient.

In return we have received official lies, ping-pong tactics from office to office, authority to authority, ministry to ministry, never so much as a word of hard decisions, only indirect instructions as for example the administration's last minute letter to the National Theater not to permit us entry on February 15, 1982. There has been no courage to address decisively or conclusively to our countless communications over a period of three months. Instead only monumental indecision and a barrage of verbal excuses to frustrate us.

The manner in which the refusal of permission to stage the play was carried out reveals a very serious element in Kenya today. The fact that the government conducted their instructions verbally or by telephone without ever writing to us directly so that no written record exists reinforces a dangerous trend. Thus acts are carried out without any officials being held accountable. Under such an atmosphere, anything can be done to any Kenyan or group of Kenyans by officials without written documentation or accountability.

This is not just simple irresponsibility and heavy-handed use of authority. The government seems mortally terrified of peasants organizing themselves on their terms and their own initiative.

We wish to denounce in the strongest possible terms the government's increasing intolerance and repression of the Kenyan people's cultural initiatives. Secondly we now question fundamentally the seriousness of the government's commitment to Kenyan culture. If, as we are told, the economy has slowed down for "external factors" of recession, inflation and petroleum prices, we ask is Kenyan culture to slow down or stagnate for the same reasons? If we had chosen to do often mindless and always irrelevant pieces as the foreign groups we probably might not have met with such official hostility. Foreign theater can freely thrive on Kenyan soil. But there is no room for Kenyan theater on Kenyan soil. During the Emergency, the British colonial regime introduced severe censorship of Kenyan theater particularly in detention camps like Athi River and employed African rehabilitation officers to do their dirty work. The similar tactics are being used in Kenya today! We now call for an end of censorship of Kenyan people's cultural expression...

I made the statement on Wednesday, March 10, 1982, on behalf of Kamiriithu Community Education and Cultural Center Theater Group. On Thursday, March 11, the government through the Provincial Commissioner for Central Province, revoked the license for Kamiriithu Community Education and Cultural Center. He said that women were being misled into cultural activities that had nothing to do with development. He therefore banned all theater activities in the area.

On Friday, March 12, the District Officer for Limuru led three truckloads of heavily armed police and demolished Kamiriithu's peoples open air theater.

The government never gave the group permission to go to Zimbabwe, where it had been invited by the Ministry of Education and Culture. Our letters to the Minister of Culture informing him about the invitation were never answered, not even acknowledged. We were unable to go to Zimbabwe.

In view of President Moi's recent public statements attacking theater at Kamiriithu, one can now definitely say that the whole cultural repression was *not* an accident or an isolated mistake of some over-zealous philistines in the provincial administration but a deliberate thought-out action of a nervous regime. The government ban on the public performance of other plays (*Muntu* by Joe de Graft; *Kilio* by students of Nairobi school, etc.) and the arrests and detentions of university teachers, students, lawyers, left-wing politicians, and the general climate of terror would confirm that the destruction of Kamiriithu was part and parcel of a programmed attempt to enforce conformity of thought on the entire population by rooting out critical elements and the suspension of the democratic process in politics, education and culture. But conformity to which thought?

It may be pointed out that at the same period that the Kenya government was suppressing *Maitu Njugira*, a musical depicting the worker and peasant resistance to colonial repression in a positive light, the same government had bought a TV film of Elspeth Huxley's autobiography *Flame Trees of Thika* and screened it in seven episodes on Kenya Television for two months. The film was made by a British Television Company and both the film and the book set in the 20s and 30s show Kenyans as part and parcel of the animal and natural landscape. They are certainly not shown as having any capacity for resistance.

What now? Is this the end of Kamiriithu? The government's repressive measures were certainly a setback to the development of a people based theater in the countryside. For this means that for the majority of women in the rural areas, the church on Sundays will remain as their only venue for cultural expresion by way of religious hymns, prayers, sermons and bible reading. For the others, alcohol will be their only means of entertainment. But despite this, I am convinced that the Kamiriithu idea can never be killed. How do you kill the right and the determination of a people to have a cultural life?

Kamiriithu has shown what peasants and workers are capable of doing in modern theatre if left alone to organize on their own terms. In their participation in the peasant and worker based theater, the Kamiriithu women have joined a long line of others who have always stood for a free united Kenya, a Kenya in which if a bean falls to the ground, it is shared among the children. This is the vision that guided the Mau Mau anticolonial movement and it is what today is guiding the Kenyan people in their anti-imperialist struggle against all forms of internal and external exploitation and oppression.

Gicaamba, the factory worker in the play *Ngaahika Ndeenda (I will marry when I want)* sums up the situation when talking to the other peasant and worker characters (both men and women) in the play:

GICAAMBA:
> The question is this:
> Who are our friends? And where are they?
> Who are our enemies? And where are they?
> Let us unite against our enemies.
> I don't need to elaborate!
> He who has ears, let him hear,
> He who has eyes, let him see.

I know only this:
We cannot end poverty by erecting a hundred churches in the village:
We cannot end poverty by erecting a hundred beer-halls in the village;
Ending up with two alcoholics.
The alcoholic of hard liquor.
The alcoholic of the rosary.
Let's rather unite in patriotic love:
Gikuyu once said:
[Sings]

> Two hands can carry a beehive,
> One man's ability is not enough,
> One finger cannot kill a louse,
> Many hands make work light.

Why did Gikuyu say those things?
Development will come from our unity.
Unity is our strength and wealth.
A day will surely come when
If a bean falls to the ground
It'll be split equally among us,
For—
[They sing]
SOLOIST:

> *The trumpet—*

ALL:

> *Of the workers has been blown*
> *To wake all the slaves*
> *To wake all the peasants*
> *To wake all the poor.*
> *To wake the masses.*

SOLOIST:

> *The trumpet—*

ALL:

> *Of the poor has been blown.*

SOLOIST:

> *The trumpet!*

ALL:

> *The trumpet of the masses has been blown.*
> *Let's preach to all our friends.*
> *The trumpet of the masses has been blown.*
> *We change to new songs*
> *For the revolution is near.*

SOLOIST:

> *The trumpet!*

ALL:

> *The trumpet of the masses has been blown.*

SOLOIST:

> *The trumpet of the masses has been blown.*

We are tired of being robbed
We are tired of exploitation
We are tired of land grabbing
We are tired of slavery
We are tired of charity and abuses.
SOLOIST:
The trumpet!
ALL:
The trumpet of the poor has been blown.
Let's unite and organize
Organization is our club
Organization is our sword
Organization is our gun
Organization is our shield
Organization is the way
Organization is our strength
Organization is our light
Organization is our wealth.
SOLOIST:
The trumpet!
ALL:
The trumpet of the masses has been blown.
SOLOIST:
The trumpet—
ALL:
Of the workers has been blown
There are two sides in the struggle,
The side of the exploiters and that of the exploited.
On which side will you be when
SOLOIST:
The trumpet—
ALL:
Of the workers is finally blown?

Like Gicaamba, the people of Kenya—men, women and children—are looking out to see who their friends are. Anybody who would raise their voice against the current cultural and political repression in the land and against the denial of Kenyans their democratic and human rights to organize in whatever capacity on their own terms are friends of Kenyan people and of democracy.

Everyone has the right to freedom of opinion and expression; says article 19 of the Universal Declaration of Human Rights. All cultural and women's organizations all over the world should raise their voices against what's happening in Kenya. Certainly they should make their abhorrence of rule by terror known to the Kenyan authorities in every venue at every opportunity. No amount of material wellbeing like giving three sewing machines to a village of 10,000 people as the authorities have recently done at Kamiriithu!) can compensate for the loss of a people's right to determine their lives or at least have a say in such a determination.

Development should mean the release of the creative powers in men, women and children. The destruction of a cultural center is an attempt to stifle creativity and it tells more about the spiritual and mental states of these regimes which nervously reach out for the pistol at the mention of the phrase people's culture. It is interesting that the authorities changed the name of the Kamiriithu Community Education and Cultural Center to Kamiriithu Polytechnic and Adult Literacy Center, while banning all theater activities in the area. At the entrance of the open air theater (now destroyed) there stood a board with the inscriptions *Muci wa muingi* in Gikuyu, and *Mji wa umma* in Kiswahili. Both phrases meant the same thing: A People's Cultural Center.

The board was the first to be removed and destroyed in the police raid of March 12, 1982. The regime can destroy people's centers and even abolish theater: but can they destroy or abolish the people? That's why I say: Kamiriithu will come back!

Ah, yes, may it come! But I'm still convinced that the biggest aid and gift to Kenyan people by their friends is a call and an insistence on Kenyan authorities to return to the democratic process by releasing the university lecturers and all other political prisoners and by lifting the ban on theater among peasants and workers.

Detention in Neocolonial Kenya

In a neocolonial country, the act of detaining patriotic democrats, progressive intellectuals and militant workers speaks of many things. It is first an admission by the detaining authorities that their official lies labelled as a new philosophy, their pretensions often hidden in three-piece suits and golden chains, their propaganda packaged as religious truth, their plastic smiles ordered from abroad, their nationally televised charitable handouts and breast-beating before the high altar, their high-sounding phrases and ready-to-shed tears at the sight of naked children fighting it out with cats and dogs for the possession of a rubbish heap, that these and more godfatherly acts of benign benevolence have been seen by the people for what they truly are: a calculated sugar-coating of an immoral sale and mortgage of a whole country and its people to Euro-American and Japanese capital for a few million dollars in Swiss banks and a few token shares in foreign companies. Their mostly vaunted morality has been exposed for what it is: the raising of beggary and charity into moral idealism. There is a newfound dignity in begging, and charity for them is twice-blessed; it deflates the recipient and inflates the giver. Nyerere once rightly compared those African regimes who dote on their neocolonial status to a prostitute who walks with proud display of the fur coat given to her by her moneyed lover. Actually the situation of a comprador neocolonial ruling class is more appropriately comparable to that of a pimp who would proudly hold down his mother to be brutally raped by foreigners, and then shout in glee: look at the shining handful of dollars I have received for my efficiency and integrity, in carrying out my part of the bargain!

But recourse to detention is above all an admission by the neocolonial ruling minority that people have started to organize to oppose them, to oppose the continued plunder of the national wealth and heritage by this shameless alliance of a few nationals and their foreign paymasters.

Thus detention more immediately means the physical removal of patriots from the people's organized struggles. Ideally, the authorities would like to put the whole community of struggling millions behind barbed-wire, as the British colonial authorities once tried to do with Kenyan people. But this would mean incarcerating labor, the true source of national wealth: what would then be left to loot? So the authorities do the simpler thing: pick one or two individuals from among the people and then loudly claim that all sins lie at the feet of these few "power hungry, misguided" and "ambitious" agitators. Note that any awakening of a people to their historic mission of liberating themselves from external and internal exploitation and repression is always seen in terms of "sin" and it is often denounced with the religious rhetoric of a wronged, self-righteous god. These agitators suddenly become devils whose removal from society is now portrayed as a divine mission. The people are otherwise innocent, simple, peace-loving, obedient, law-abiding, and cannot conceivably harbor any desire to change this best of all possible worlds. It is partly self-deception, but also an attempted deception of millions. Chain the devils!

But political detention, not disregarding its punitive aspects, serves a deeper, exemplary ritual symbolism. If they can break such a patriot, if they can make him come out of detention crying "I am sorry for all my sins," such an unprincipled about-face would confirm the wisdom of the ruling clique in its division of the populace into the passive innocent millions and the disgruntled subversive few.

The fact is that detention without trial is not only a punitive act of physical and mental torture of a few patriotic individuals, but it is also a calculated act of psychological terror against the struggling millions. It is a terrorist program for the psychological siege of the whole nation.

From *Detained* by Ngugi wa Thiong'o,
published by Heinemann Educational Books

Freedom of the Artist:

People's Artists Versus People's Rulers

In its origins, the word *art* meant science, knowledge, or learning. But it now connotes more than that: it refers not to learning and knowledge simply but to learning and knowledge in ways different from those associated with science. Art is a way of seeing, or apprehending, the world of man and nature through visual, sound or mental images. Through these images, the whole conglomerate of skills that we call *art* or the *arts* assault our consciousness to make us take a certain view of the World of Man and Nature. Let me illustrate this with a few examples.

In the *Daily Nation* of July 10, 1980, there was a letter from a Zarina Patel, Mombasa, calling upon the authorities to name the bridge linking Mombasa to the North mainland, Me Katilili Bridge. The following is the picture she painted of this Kenyan nationalist leader:

> Me Katilili has a very important place in the history of Kenya's Coast Province. She was a Giriama who fought courageously and relentlessly against the British colonial forces in the early part of this century. She and the warriors whom she led refused to accept British imperialist subjugation and exploitation. They attacked the colonialists at every possible opportunity. Finally in 1914, the British with their superior weaponry, captured Me Katilili. So powerful and influential was she that they had to deport her out of the area. It is time we at the Coast requested the government to recognize concretely the nationalism and bravery of Me Katilili.

That is how a Kenyan patriot has described Me Katilili. But in another description written on November 23, 1913, the British Colonial District Commissioner, Arthur M. Champion, paints a very different picture of Me Katilili's organized resistance to British imperialist occupation.

> The witch Me Katilili and the witch doctor Wanji wa Mandora about the

end of June 1913 did stir up sedition amongst the natives . . . and with this object held a large gathering of men determined to make a common cause with (other) disaffected natives . . . to meat a spell or Kiroho for the purpose of defeating a successful Government Administration . . . I would therefore recommend that both the woman Me Katilili and Wanji Wa Mandora be deported from the district and be detained as political prisoners at His Majesty's pleasure.

Thus to a Kenyan, Me Katilili is a nationalist who heroically resisted the British occupation of Kenya: to the British imperialist, she is a witch. In Zarina's description, acts of resistance to foreign occupation are linked to qualities of courage and heroism which deserve national recognition and pride. To Champion, acts of resistance to foreign occupation are linked to negative qualities of witchcraft and savagery. Both have used word images to persuade us or make us unconsciously or consciously take a certain attitude to Me Katilili and to imperialism: resistance to imperialism is good, noble, heroic—Zarina's nationalist patriotic view; acquiescence and accommodation to imperialism is good, noble—Champion's colonialist's view.

If you have read Haggard's *King Solomon's Mines* you'll have seen how another African woman leader of resistance against the British occupation of South Africa is described: Gagool is a most revolting picture of a human being. But the same type of medicine man in the character of Mkomozi is painted very differently but positively in Peter Abraham's novel *The Wild Conquest*. In Karen Blixen's (Isak Dinesen's) book *Out of . Africa*, all Kenyans are described in terms of beasts utterly divorced from civilization. This is her description of Kamante, her cook.

Kamante could have no idea as to how a dish of ours ought to taste, and he was, in spite of his conversion, and his connection with civilization, at heart an arrant Kikuyu . . . He did at times taste the food that he cooked, but then with a distrustful face, like a witch who takes a sip out of her cauldron. He stuck to the maize cobs of his forefathers. Here even his intelligence failed him and he came and offered me a Kikuyu delicacy of a roasted sweet potato or a lump of sheep's fat—as even a civilized dog, that has lived for a long time with people, will place a bone on the floor before you, as a present.

Out of Africa was first published in 1937. Karen Blixen was describing the life of Kenyans whom she had robbed of vast acres of land near Ngong Hills. Jomo Kenyatta's *Facing Mount Kenya* was first published in 1938. He concludes thus:

As it is, by driving him off his ancestral lands, the Europeans have robbed him (the Kenyan) of the material foundations of his culture, and reduced him to a state of serfdom incompatible with human happiness. The African is conditioned, by the cultural and social institutions of centuries, to a freedom of which Europe has little conception, and it is not in his nature to

> accept serfdom forever. He realizes that he must fight unceasingly for his complete emancipation; for without this, he is doomed to remain the prey of rival imperialisms, which in every successive year will drive their fangs more deeply into his vitality and strength.

Well, two very different images of the Kenyan realities under colonial rule: to Karen Blixen, Kenyans are dogs and colonialists are gods; to Kenyatta, a Kenyan is a civilized being and the colonialist is a beast of prey with bloody fangs.

In religious art you'll find that colonialist paintings tend to depict Satan as a black man with two horns and a tail with one leg raised in a dance of savagery: God is a white man with rays of light radiating from his face. But to the African, the colonialist was a devil, a *Mzungu hasa*, for he had no human skin.

It is the same story in cinematic arts and even in music: assault our consciousness by giving us certain images of social realities. The musical arts are even more direct in their impact on the consciousness: certain songs create a sense of fear, of an impending doom, while others, like those used in the recent Tamaduni production of *Mzalendo Kimathi* (the Swahili translation of *The Trial of Dedan Kimathi*) create a mood of patriotic courage and anti-imperialist defiance. Missionary Christian songs created a mood of passivity and acceptance—*"Ndi Mwihia o na wanyona"* ("I'm a sinner") or "Wash me redeemer and I shall be whiter than snow," cried the African convert to his Maker. Liberation music created a joyous aggressive mood, a sense of inevitable triumph over the enemy—"Twathiiaga tukeneete, tugacooka o tukeneete" ("We joyfully and fearlessly went to battle"), or "When our Kimaathi ascended the mountain he asked for courage and strength to defeat the British imperialist," so sang the Mau Mau guerrilla fighter as he went to fight in the forest. Both the Christian colonialist and the resistance music sang of the same reality—the foreign occupation of Kenya—but from two conflicting opposed perspectives.

The arts then are a form of knowledge about reality acquired through a pile of images. But these images are not neutral. The images given us by the arts try to make us not only see and understand the world of man and nature, apprehend it, but to see and understand it in a certain way, or from the angle of vision of the artist. The *way* or the *angle of vision* is itself largely affected by the margin of natural, social and spiritual freedom within which the practitioner of the skills (the writer, the musician, the painter) is operating.

Let me put it another way. The arts present us with a set of images of the world in which we live. The arts then act like a reflecting mirror. The artist is like the hand that holds and moves the mirror, this way and that way, to explore all corners of the universe. But what is reflected in the mirror depends on where the holder stands in relation to the object. Other factors come into it too: whether or not the hand has chosen, consciously or unconsciously, a concave or convex mirror, a broken or an unbroken mirror. Any factor or factors that limit the capacity of the mirror to give us correct and illuminating images of the world are themselves limitations on the exploring hand, the hand of the artist, and they have to do with the margin of natural, economic, political, social and spiritual freedom within which the explorer is operating. These factors may or may not be internal or external to the artist. Or they may be both internal and external.

So while there are many ways of approaching this difficult problem of the freedom of the artist, I shall pose three questions around which I shall introduce a discussion on the issue:

1. Has the artist equipped himself with a world view which enables him to see as much of the world as it is possible for him to see and to make us see? For as charity begins at home so must the freedom of the artist: has he or not first accepted to liberate himself from certain inhibiting angles of vision? In other words can an artist adopt and defend the viewpoing of an oppressing class and be free? Were Karen Blixen, Elspeth Huxley, Robert Ruark really free when they put their art to the service of imperialist exploitation and oppression of Kenyans? And here we can compare the limitations of these artists with the largeness of vision of artists like Balzac or Tolstoy who, although they came from oppressing classes, distanced themselves sufficiently to see and expose the reality of brutality behind both bouregois and feudal class dictatorships.

Brecht, in a poem called *Driven out with Good Reason*, could as easily have been describing a Tolstoy or a Balzac when he wrote:

> I grew up as the son
> of well-to-do people. My parents put
> A collar round my neck and brought me up
> In the habit of being waited on
> And schooled me in the art of giving orders. But
> When I was grown up and looked about me
> I did not like the people of my own class
> Nor giving orders, nor being waited on
> And I left my own class and allied myself
> With insignificant people.
> Thus
> They brought up a traitor, taught him
> All their tricks, and he
> Betrayed them to the enemy.
> Yes, I give away their secrets. I stand
> Among the people and explain

Their swindles. I say in advance what will happen, for I
Have inside knowledge of their plans.
The Latin of their corrupt clergy
I translate word for word into the common speech, and then
It is seen to be humbug. The scales of their justice
I take down so as to show
The fraudulent weights. And their informers report
to them
That I sit among the dispossessed when they
Are plotting rebellion.

Will the artist choose the angle of vision of the possessing classes? Or will he choose the angle of vision of the dispossessed and therefore struggling classes? Each artist has to make a choice. For this is the area of spiritual freedom. Or call it the area of self-liberation!

2. Is the artist operating in a situation in which he is continually being harassed by the state, or continually under the threat of such a harassment? Has he the democratic rights to practice his art without fear of state intervention by way of censorship or prisons or detention camps? Even if the artist is not actually placed in a Maximum Security Prison for a year or more, is he really free when he practices self-censorship for the very well founded fears of such an eventuality? This is the area of democratic freedom.

3. Is he operating within an inhibiting social structure of all social systems? In other words, even if an artist had adopted a world view that allows him to see all, and he had the democratic right to say it how he will without fear of certain death or prison, is he free in a class structured society where a few give orders and the majority obey, where a million toil and only a few reap? Is he free for as long as he is, for instance, living in an imperialist dominated world where the "third" world peoples produce and the barons of profit in New York, Bonn, London, Paris, Stockholm, Rome and Tokyo dispose? Here we are talking of much more than the freedom of the artist: we are talking about the freedom of all the toiling masses as the very condition of a true creative freedom! This is the area of human freedom to be free to become even more human: the freedom of human labor, the final artist! In the case of us Kenyans can an artist be free for as long as our economy and culture are dominated by imperialist foreigners and their local allies?

Let me briefly examine the three areas of an artist's freedom.

1. Throughout history, there have been two conflicting world views. The first view sees the world of nature and man as static and fixed. Or if it moves at all, it is in cycles, repetitive of the same motions. Any concession to evidence or demonstration of previous movement in history is twisted to prove that the logic in all the previous movements was to ar-

rive at the present fixed status quo. This is the world view of all the ruling classes in all hitherto class-structured societies: We have arrived at the best of all possible worlds. A few examples will do:

(a) The feudal ruling classes in Europe for centuries held to the Ptolemic view of the universe: that the earth was fixed and all the stars including the sun revolved round the earth with the feudal monarchs and clergy at the center. People arguing against this were burnt alive as heretics; how could they question that which was sanctioned by God?

(b) The British ruling classes said that the slave system (selling and buying Africans, that is) which produced such profitable sugar, tobacco and cotton, was the best of all possible social systems for the slave (he now had a chance of acquiring a Christian name, James or Charles) and for the slave dealer: he could bank his millions on earth and buy a mansion in heaven for afterlife.

(c) The U.S. ruling circles will concede that there was a time when colonialism was not quite so good for Euro-Americans and they fought for independence from London. Every July 4, they pay annual tribute to their forefathers who fought for an America free from British colonial rule. But now that U.S. imperialism dominates and rules most of Africa, Latin America and Asia, they argue that the world has arrived at the final system: the rule of financial monopoly capital guaranteed by American guns and yellow corn!

(d) And finally some well placed Kenyans will concede that the different precolonial stages of communal and feudal developments in Kenya caved in to the colonial stage of imperialism: that patriotic Kenyans in turn fought bravely to end the colonial stage of imperialist domination. But since the midnight of December 12, 1963, we have arrived at the best of all possible world systems!

The second world view sees that movement (or change) is inherent in nature and society. In this view, nature and society are in perpetual motion; that nothing is really static, fixed, final. Life is motion and motion is life. In this view, no social system is really final and fixed but each contains the germs of a future society. But motion involves contradictions for as Blake once stated without contrariness there is no progression. This broadly is the world view of the downtrodden, of the oppressed, of the dominated: change is inevitable even if it does not necessarily occur in a smooth line from one stage to the other.

The two world views have been in mortal conflict for the old never willingly gives place to the new. Those who profit from the old do not want anything that would disturb what they see as a well founded stability.

This conflict is well captured by Bertolt Brecht in his play the *Life of Galileo* in which he dramatizes the struggle between the Ptolemic and the Copernican systems. Galileo, a great mathematician, philosopher and astronomer, is able to demonstrate by a newly invented telescope that the earth is not the fixed center of the universe, that the sun does not in fact move round the earth. At one stage he goes back to Florence naively believing that once the Pope and all the defenders of the old system look into the telescope, then they would see the proof with their own eyes and abandon the old views about the immutability of the universe. Some look through the telescope but refuse to believe the evidence. Others refuse to even look, which drives Galileo to plead with them: "Gentlemen, I beseech you in all humility to trust the evidence of your eyes." It is one of Galileo's friends who tells him the truth:

> Galileo, I see you setting out on a fearful road. It is a night of disaster when a man sees the truth. And an hour of delusion when he believes in the common sense of the human race . . . How could those in power leave at large a man who knows the truth, even though it be about the most distant stars? Do you think the Pope will hearken to your truth when you say he is in error? . . . . Do you think that *he* will simply write in his diary: January the tenth, 1610—Heaven abolished?

What is at stake as Galileo discovers late is not the truth about the movement of distant stars, but the threat to the feudal system of inequality, corruption, oppression and privileges of which the ptolemic view was a mere philosophic defense and rationale.

In other words the world view that nothing ever changes suits those profiting from the social status quo: "Good Morning Mr. Dispossessed," says Mr. Possessing. "A bad morning," replies Mr. Dispossessed. "I'm truly sorry about your condition," adds Mr. Possessing. "But it's you who is sitting on my back," replies Mr. Dispossessed. "That's the Law of Nature and God," says Mr. Possessing, adding helpfully, "Let's all live in harmony and brotherly togetherness. Let's not disturb the universal law of stability." Tolstoy has put it succinctly:

> I sit on a man's back choking him
> and making him carry me, and yet assure myself and others
> that I am very sorry for him and
> wish to ease his lot by any
> means possible except getting
> off his back.

But Mr. Dispossessed is not likely to accept that being sat upon is in accordance with a fixed law of God and Nature. The world view corresponding to his objective position of wanting the burden off his back is the one that says that motion (or change) is inherent in nature and human society.

The two world views have produced two types of artists: the poet laureate or the court singer to the status quo, and the trumpeter of a new world. The first type is not really free, he is in a state of self-imposed slavery, while the second type is free of illusions about the present because his adopted world view—that change with all the contradictions involved is inevitable—has liberated his faculties of observation.

2. But when we come to the area of political or democratic freedom the situation of the two types of artists changes. He who holds the world view of the ruling classes is free to write, to sing, to paint, to dance the dance of the times. The spiritual slave becomes free to sing virtues of slavery and is given accolades for it. But the artist with a questioning spirit, the trumpeter of possibilities of a better social order, now becomes unfree to write, to sing, to paint, to dance about the heralds of a new dawn. If he should persist in his heretical position, he is persecuted, accused of a thousand and one crimes. Socrates was accused of corrupting the youth of Greece and he was hounded to death.

Aristotle at one time had to flee into exile arguing: "We shall not let Athens offend twice against philosophy."

Galileo had to publicly abjure or recant what he knew to be the truth. Those three—death, exile or renouncing the truth—are often the cruel choices open to the second type of artist.

I am not of course suggesting that if an artist has not been killed, or jailed or exiled or has had his works banned, then he does not belong to the second category of artists. You may perhaps know the amusing poem of Bertolt Brecht on the burning of books: A certain regime once commanded that all books with harmful knowledge should be publicly burned. But one of the best writers, moreover one who had been in trouble with the regime to the extent of being exiled, happened to see the list of books put to the bonfire and he was shocked to find that his books were not on the list.

> He rushed to his desk
> on wings of wrath, and wrote a letter to those in power
> Burn me! he wrote with flying pen, burn me!
> Haven't my books
> Always reported the truth? And here you are
> Treating me like a liar! I command you:
> Burn me!

So I am not asking that African artists rush to the authorities and say "please persecute me" for this is not necessarily a proof that the artist is painting images of truth.

Nevertheless I would like to illustrate the state of the relative freedom and unfreedom of the two types of artists by quickly looking at Kenya's record in this matter both before and after independence.

All the writers, dramatists, actors, dancers and singers who supported colonialist oppression and exploitation of Kenyans by the British imperialist bourgoisie and its local Kenya settler representatives were always free to practice their art. Karen Blixen could describe Kenyans as dogs, hyenas, jackals and the like and be canonized for it: She was once a likely recipient of the Nobel Prize for Literature. In her book of memoirs *Shadows on the Grass* published in 1960, three years before Kenya's independence, she could still write about Kenyans in terms of beasts of burden.

> The dark nations of Africa, strikingly precocious as young children, seemed to come to a standstill in their mental growth at different ages. The Kikuyu, Kawirondo, and Wakamba, the people who worked for me on the farm, in early childhood were far ahead of white children of the same age, but they stopped quite suddenly at a stage corresponding to that of a European child of nine. The Somali had got further and had all the mentality of boys of our own race at the age of 13 to 17.

Today independent Kenya still honors her name by naming a whole district in Nairobi after her. Karen is still one of the most fashionable residential areas in the city.

Elspeth Huxley, who depicted Kenyans as children perpetually amazed at airplanes and razor blades, was always on every Royal Commission of Inquiry into grievances of natives—whether on land or education matters. Her latest book, *Nellie*, in which she describes Mau Mau Freedom Fighters as beasts, is currently a best seller in Nairobi bookshops. The present Kenyan authorities allowed the film of her racist memoirs, *The Flame Trees of Thika*, to be shot in Kenya and when the film is done, I have no doubts it will be shown in Nairobi cinemas.

Robert Ruak, who always described Kenyan Africans as wogs in his two anti-Mau Mau novels *Something of Value* and *Uhuru*, was the he-man version of Hemingway in Kenya. His books still grace the shelves of our libraries and bookshops.

The same story is true of theater: European colonial theater has thrived on such stages as Little Theater in Mombasa, Donvon Maule Theater in Nairobi, the Kenya National Theater and other theaters in Nakuru and Eldoret, since the fifties.

Among Africans, those who sang and composed Christian songs in praise of a white God were always free to do so a thousand times over. A colonial government commissioned an African artist to paint some murals in a church in Murang'a in memory of those Kenyans who opposed the Mau Mau struggle. He went ahead with the grand task. In detention camps, those singing Christian songs and writing Christian pro-colonial plays—what J.M. Kariuki once described as Marebe Theater—were free to do so. In fact, they were very highly encouraged and rewarded for their anti-Kenyan artistic efforts.

The story changes when we come to the patriotic artistic tradition

Freedom of the Artist

among Kenyans.

About 1930, the *Ituika* revolutionary Cultural Festival among the aagikuyu was banned. This was a festival of songs, dances, poetry and theater that took place every 25 years as a memorial to an earlier revolutionary overthrow of a feudal dictatorship by the Iregi generation.

At about the same period the Muthirigu dancers, composers and singers were banned with most being hounded to jails. Their songs and dances were anti-imperialist and they talked of a new Kenya to come. It's the same story about Mumboist artists and those associated with the anticolonial *dini Ya Musambwa* movement. Is there in Kenya today any shrine erected in honor of Muthoni Nyanjiru who sang of a new Kenya even as she was mowed down by colonialist bullets outside the Norfolk Hotel on the very grounds this university stands?

But the repression of patriotic Kenyan literature and the arts reached its climax in the fifties. Mau Mau publishing houses, Mau Mau poetry and songs and drama were banned. Writers and publishers of this patriotic literature like Gakaara Wanjau and Kimuthia Mugia were hounded to detention camps in Manyani. Kenya's patriotic theater, like Kimathi's Gicamu Theater movement in Karuna-ini were either banned, or stopped under the general colonialist violence and repression in the land. In place of this, the colonial government appointed an European Kenyan-wide drama and music officer, Mr. Graham Hyslope, to channel Kenyan African drama and music into idiotic directions of pointless clowning and drumming in community halls, schools and churches. I could extend the same story to journalists: freedom and honor for those in praise of colonialism, jail, detention or exile for patriotic ones.

I am afraid that the political fate of the two types of artists has not been very different in an independent Kenya.

European and foreign theater, even when it has been racist and anti-Kenyan, has flourished freely, often under government protection. In the process some European theater critics have become so arrogant that one of them, Mary Hayne, had the audacity as late as 1979 to write in a Kenyan newspaper describing Kimathi as a terrorist.

Foreign, particularly European, music is the order of the day in Kenyan churches and schools. Can we imagine the amount of money the Kenyan government is spending in organizing the current primary schools' music competition? And this in order that impressionable Kenyan children shall sing in praise of a rich White Lady riding a White Horse:

> Riding on a horse
> To Banbury Cross
> To see a White Lady
> Ride on a White Horse
> With rings on her fingers

> And bells on her toes,
> She shall have music
> Wherever she goes.

When I myself used to write plays and novels that were only critical of the racism in the colonial system, I was praised. I was awarded prizes, and my novels were in the syllabus. But when toward the seventies I started writing in a language understood by peasants, and in an idiom understood by them and I started questioning the very foundations of imperialism and of foreign domination of Kenya economy and culture, I was sent to Kamiti Maximum Security Prison.

But it's wrong, as *The African Perspective* of February-March 1978 was to claim, that I was the first writer to be jailed in an independent Kenya:

> Ngugi's own detention came as a shock because of Kenya's enviable record in this regard. The government has always allowed its intellectuals the freedom to express their criticisms of society as it is presently constituted and no writer or artist has ever been jailed, with or without trial.

The great Kenyan poet Abdilatif Abdalla, the author of *Sauti Ya Dhiki*, was jailed for three years at Kamiti Maximum Security Prison (between 1969 and 1972) for writing a pamphlet simply asking: *Kenya: Twendapi? (Kenya, where are we heading to?)*. *The African Perspective* was also wrong implying that I was the first artist whose freedom of expression had been curtailed by the government. Richard Frost, in his unwittingly illuminating book about the working of cultural imperialism in Kenya called *Race Against Time*, cites, though in praise, one of the earliest cases of artistic suppression:

> A month of two before independence the members of an African boys' club in one of the poorest districts of Nairobi wrote a play which they wanted to act in the Uhuru Stadium during the Independence celebrations or, if that were not possible, on successive evenings in the social halls in the various parts of the city. The play was an ignorant travesty of history and was intended to create hatred of Britain and the colonial administration. The matter was brought to the attention of Tom Mboya, the minister responsible for the independence celebrations. He asked to see the script and immediately banned its performance anywhere. "That," he said, "is not the spirit in which we want to enter independence."

The suppression of Kenya artists in post-independence Kenya is contained in a Kenya Writers' Association Memorandum on the status of the artist submitted to UNESCO. I will not go into details but I could mention a few cases: Micere Githae Mugo (poet, playwright, short-story writer, critic) was in 1977 arrested and tortured in police cells. Ngugi wa Mirii (composer, playwright) has lost his job with the University of Nairobi. Many Kenyan journalists have been locked up in police cells or questioned for their critical writings and exposure.

Freedom of the Artist

But there's one case which should come to the eyes of the Kenyan Public and the concerned authorities and which ought to be the concern of every Kenyan patriot. I am referring to those girls from Riara Loreto Secondary School in Kaimbu District who in 1979 wrote a play: *What a World My People!* or *There Are Two Worlds.* Under the patronage of their brilliant drama teacher, Sister Agnes Wanjiku Mukabi, they wrote and produced the play for the 1979 Kenya Drama School Festival. It won several regional prizes before being "defeated" at the provincial level. But the play was sufficiently popular for it to be demanded by several schools and colleges around. I understand that it was even performed at the Kenyatta College Cultural Festival, which was launched by President Moi in 1979. But when the girls translated the play into Gikuyu language and performed to their peasant parents, the police moved in, questioned the headmistress and the drama teacher, and the play was subsequently stopped. Now I understand that five or seven of the girls involved in the play, including the author, were later expelled from the school. I understand that the Catholic Church hierarchy was not slow in following the lead. The drama teacher, a nun, was not allowed to take her final vows, she was unceremoniously thrown out of the Catholic order and shipped to America.

I ask myself: What effect has this kind of action had on the creative development of such children? Should such a tremendous initiative by mere Form Three girls have been encouraged or suppressed? And this at a time when imperialist theater, foreign critics, foreign music are being actively encouraged. Even foreign embassies are more free to organize Kenyan theater, art and music on our own soil than patriotic Kenyans themselves!

What we are asking for is very simple: Not that the Karen Blixens, the Elspeth Huxleys and the foreign theater groups be stopped. No, we are not asking for special state protection, but that Kenya patriotic theater be not suppressed. Let a hundred schools of drama contend in the villages, in the cities, in the schools and colleges and we shall see which will win the day. I do not need to be a prophet to say that foreign music, foreign cinema, foreign art has no future in this country no matter the amount of freedom and state patronage it is accorded. But why should an African government in an independent Kenya see its role as that of protecting foreign antinational interests and suppressing voices of Kenyan people? Allow your strip-tease artists, your Elspeth Huxleys, your *Dallas* television programs and so on, but let Kenyans also get equal freedom.

But in another sense Kenyan artists are themselves to blame for their present plight because of their complacency and indifference to their democratic rights as Kenyans. We have in the past adopted the attitude: Every one for himself and even a separate God for each of us. We have never come together to voice those interests that bind us together as Kenyan patriotic artists. Do we as writers, musicians, painters, expect engineers to come out and speak for our legitimate self-interests? Democracy is possible only when various self-interest groups in the country, whatever their outlook, begin to voice their legitimate self-interests as groups. Only on that basis can there even be a dialogue about the freedom of the artist.

There is a poem by Martin Niemoeller which should be of interest to all those desirous of an extension of democratic rights to artistic expression:

To the Faculty

In Germany they first come for the communists and I did not speak up
    because I wasn't a communist.
Then they came for the Jews and I did not speak up because I wasn't a Jew.
Then they came for the trade unionists and I did not speak up because I
    wasn't a trade unionist.
They they came for the catholics and I didn't speak up because I was a
    protestant.
Then they came for me—and by that timeno one was left to speak up.

Let us Kenyan artists in unison raise all our voices against repression of artists and our cultural initiatives. Now!

3. Finally I want to be very brief on the third area of an artist's freedom. Even if a writer or an artist had a liberated vision and was allowed to write freely, can he be said to be free when the very society in which he lives is a class structured society with a few living on the labor of millions? The artist to the extent that he is a member of a given society is caught up in the contradictions of that society. In the advanced Western capitalist democracies, many artists, unable to face the extreme contradictions of capitalism and the impoverishment of human life under the same economic system, have been driven to individualism, cynicism, abstractionism, despair and often suicide. In the branch capitalisms of the third world countries, the contradictions are multiplied: not only is there internal exploitation and oppression but there is external exploitation and oppression of the whole nation by the imperialist bourgeoisie. In such a situation, no artist can consider himself free for the condition of his freedom is the freedom of the vast majority of the population.

Let me put it another way. The real artist in the world is human labor. It's human labor which has created the social environment out of the natural environment. All the modern technology and science and the arts are a product of human labor. When the product of that social human labor becomes the property of an idle few, can the artist be said to be free? And remember that the situation is worse when the products of the human labor of a given country are controlled by foreigners. The liberation of human labor is the only condition for the true liberation of the human being, the artist.

For the Kenya artist, the most minimal step towards his own freedom is a total immersion in the struggles of Kenyan workers and peasants for the liberation of the products of their labor for the benefit of Kenyans. Imperialist foreign domination of a people's economy and culture is completely incompatible with the freedom of the artist in the third world.

Here we come to another contradiction. For it is precisely the artist who realizes the need to struggle against foreign imperialist domination and against every form of internal and external exploitation and oppression who is likely to find himself without the democratic freedom to express this. In other words, it is precisely this kind of artist who is likely to be persecuted to cower him into succumbing to a neocolonial culture of silence and fear. But in this, the persecuting authorities are mistaken. It is very difficult to suppress the truth. There is a legend that as Galileo rose from his knees after he had abjured and sworn that the earth did not turn round the sun, he nevertheless muttered: "Yet it does turn." After the Kenyan poet Abdilatif Abdalla was imprisoned, he came out of jail and published *Sauti Ya Dhiki* in which he writes:

> Kweli ilipowatoma, kama dasturi yake
> Wao wakaona vyema, afadhali wanishike
> Wanishike hima hima, hima ndani waniweke
> Ngomeni n'adhibike, nijute kusema kweli

And virtually each verse of the opening poem ends with defiant refrain: *N'shishiyelo ni Lilo* (The truth I held, I still hold on to even more firmly.)

Abdilatif's defiant position is reminiscent of the Palestinian poet Mahmoud Darwish who in his poem *On Man* in his book *The Music of Human Flesh* has written the following lines of defiant immortality:

> Oh you with bloodshot-eyes and bloody hands
> Night is short lived,
> The detention room lasts not for ever,
> Nor yet the links of chain.

Abdilatif and Darwish are right: the correct response to those who would butcher life and truth is defiance. The only answer to fascism is resistance. Fascism, autocracy, authoritarianism, work by striking fear in the population to scatter organized opposition. Therefore the first thing to resist is fear itself.

There is a fine instructive poem by Brecht on Hitler's Germany, *Anxieties of the Regime.*

> A foreigner, returning from a trip to the Third Reich
> When asked who really ruled there, answered:

Fear.
Anxiously
The scholar breaks off his discussion to inspect
The thin partitions of his study, his face ashen. The teacher
Lies sleepless, worrying over
An ambiguous phrase the inspector had let fall.
The old woman in the grocer's shop
Put her trembling finger to her lips to hold back
Her angry exclamation about the bad flour. Anxiously
The doctor inspects the strangulation marks on his patient's throat.
Full of anxiety, parents look at their children as at traitors.
Even the dying
Hush their failing voices as they
Take leave of their relatives.
But likewise the brownshirts themselves
Fear the man whose arm doesn't fly up
And are terrified of the man who
Wishes them a good morning.
The shrill voices of those who give orders
Are full of fear like the squeaking of
Piglets awaiting the butcher's knife, as their fat arses
Sweat with anxiety in their office chairs.
Driven by anxiety
They break into homes and search the lavatories
And it is anxiety
That makes them burn whole libraries. Thus
Fear rules not only those who are ruled, but
the rulers too.

Our pens should be used to increase the anxieties of all oppressive regimes. At the very least the pen should be used to "murder their sleep" by constantly reminding them of their crimes against the people, and making them know that they are being seen. The pen may not always be mightier than the sword, but used in the service of truth, it can be a mighty force. It's for the writers themselves to choose whether they will use their art in the service of the exploiting oppressing classes and nations articulating their world view or in the service of the masses engaged in a fierce struggle against human degradation and oppression. But I have indicated my preference: Let our pens be the voices of the people. Let our pens give voices to silence.

For the artist who has chosen the side of the struggling millions, he or she should work in a strong organization with others of his kind to ensure the maximum freedom for the hand that moves the pen.

Freedom, even for the artist, was never given on a silver platter.

Writing for Peace *

There are certain images in literature, especially children's literature, which live long in one's memory. The encounter between Sindbad and the old man of the sea, for instance, has always haunted me. You know the story. Sindbad finds an old man unable to cross the river and he has pity on him. He carries him on his back. But the old man refuses to get off and instead plants his long nails even more deeply into Sindbad. The sailor grows thin even as the old man waxes fat and oozes comfort. For it is Sindbad who does everything: he carries and feeds the old man in sun and rain and wind.

I was born in a colonial situation and I suppose the image of the parasitic old man sitting and feeding on Sindbad reflected a certain reality that I then only vaguely understood. Now I know. Sindbad is from the underdeveloped world politely referred to as the developing or the third world. The old man could come from anywhere—Europe, America or Japan—but his contemporary home is the United States and he has the nuclear-armed Ronald Reagan for a president. Can there ever be peace between the two, that is, as long as the old man of the sea has his blood-sucking nails deep into the other's veins?

The question is pertinent and there is no contemporary 'third' world writer who can afford to be indifferent to it or to issues of war and peace today. His historical memory would have to be too short for him not to remember that the last two world wars dragged thousands and thousands of third world peoples into an ocean of blood man-made in Europe. The two wars were fought largely to determine which European ruling class would control the lion's share of the resources of Africa and Asia. The wars were fought to see which robber would have the monopoly of robbing Africa and Asia in peace. In other words, the third world peoples were the objects and subjects of a war whose origins, conduct and outcome they were not in a position to control or influence. For then, most of Asia and Africa was under direct European economic exploitation, political oppression and cultural domination.

The situation has not changed much today. Despite formal independence most Asian, African and South American countries are still under foreign economic exploitation, political control and cultural domination and there is every reason to believe that World War III will be fought over who should control the resources of the third world. It is not an accident that most of the "trouble spots" in the world—South Korea, South Africa, the Middle East, Malvinas/Falklands to name but a few—are all within Asia, Africa and South America.

What is the effect of this domination on the Sindbads of the developing world? On the international level, the imperialist nations continue robbing the countries they dominate. They wax fatter and fatter even as their victims grow thinner and thinner. The economic gap between the two grows bigger and bigger. The third world countries have not developed independent national economies: instead they have become economic satellites of the imperialist nations. Economic satellites necessarily become political dependencies. The ruling regimes in places like Kenya and South Korea have, for instance, ceded their territories to the ruling authorities in America for military use. By ceding their territories for American military use, they put the entire population in the frontline in any nuclear confrontation involving the USA. And yet these regimes which have sold their entire populations to America—their people will die so that Americans might live—have not the slightest influence on U.S. policies. They will go along with the whimsies of whoever is placed in the White House by the dollar wielding gnomes of Wall Street.

Culturally these dependencies become ridiculous imitations of the way of life of the ruling class of the exploiting nations. Prostitution, for instance, has become a way of life labelled tourism. The U.S. military personnel must have their amusement parks and beaches and night clubs. Indeed these satellite states have put their entire womenfolk in the market for foreigners holding dollars, sterling, francs, marks or yens.

Internally, that is within the independent nation, a corrupt regime wields power. This clique grows wealthy out of the handshake it gets for its services as an intermediary between the imperialist bourgeois and its people. Massive impoverishment of the peasantry and the working population becomes the hallmark of the nation. Hunger, disease and ignorance become chronic. Politically the ruling regimes become even more detached from the people and they can only maintain power by jailing and murdering their democratic opponents; by ruthlessly suppressing any democratic dissent; and terrorizing through the military the entire population. Culturally the ruling regimes in these satellites see their mission as that of carefully preserving feudal backward traditions that enhance superstition, or else suppressing any progressive popular cultural expressions to the extent of actually destroying people's cultural centers.

It is important to stress that these regimes, completely antinational and antipeople, derive their strength from the military and so-called economic "aid" they receive from Euro-American ruling circles. They are propped up from Bonn, Paris, London and New York. The massive military aid they get is not for use against the enemies of the nation—for the enemy of the nation is the internal and external exploiter—but against internal democratic dissent. The military dictatorships in Africa, Asia and Latin America are the creation of Euro-American and Japanese imperialism. Violence is inherent in the present unequal relationship between the third world and Japan and Euro-America. Their peace is enforced by the gun, nuclear weapons even, to create stability for the dollar to make more dollars out of the working population of the dependent nations.

So the third world peoples are doubly exploited and oppressed. They must over-feed, over-clothe and over-house both the home and the foreign ruling classes. The erstwhile colony has become a neocolony and the same patterns of domination and oppression continue.

But lest those who come from the dominating countries rest complacent, they should remember that neocolonial relations can be developed even between states that used to own colonies or were formerly independent. A good example is the way Western Europe is gradually becoming a virtual satellite of America, putting their entire population and territories at the service of a trigger happy nuclear armed authority in Washington. America is prepared to fight a nuclear war to the last European and the last man in the third world.

There are at least three possible responses to the possibilities of peace in the situation of a Sindbad and the old man of the sea—that is in the situation of the exploiter and the exploited, the oppressor and the oppressed, the dominating and the dominated.

There is the conservative approach—peace through the preservation of the status quo. This is "peace" erected on slavery and it is peace only to the oppressing class or nation. It is peace or stability of the rider and the horse and I guess that this is not the kind of peace that this gathering of writers is advocating. But it is the position held by the U.S. Hence the support that the Reagan regime gives to all the brutal ruling regimes in the world. South Africa and Israel, to give just two examples, are two of the most oppressive regimes in history. They are, as you know, the only two countries in the world whose constitutions are openly and explicitly based on racism.

There is the liberal response. This position was best articulated by Tolstoy when he talked of the man who is carried on another's back and who will vehemently protest his willingness to do anything to help his victim, everything that is, except getting off his back. The advocates of mere aid-giving are in this category. The basic question is not that of aid or lack of aid to the underdeveloped world, but that of getting off their backs so they can develop national economies and hence an independent political line and culture.

There is finally the radical response. This calls for a total transformation of the systems of inequality and oppression in every nation and between nations. Modern industry, science and technology were they not directed toward maintaining inequalities (imagine the billions spent on nuclear and conventional arms!) could transform the lives of millions on earth. This response involves, at the very least, an uncompromising opposition to U.S.-led imperialism which is today the cause of both internal inequalities in the third world and between the third world as a whole and imperialist nations.

I myself do not believe that peace is possible in an imperialist dominated world. Countries struggling for their independence like Namibia; nations struggling for their liberation as in South Africa and Palestine; people struggling for a revolutionary transformation of their lives—these have no alternative but to use any means at their disposal to bring about change; and they should be supported by all those who would like to see peace as the social basis and climate for a truly human community. Here, it seems to me, the European writer has a special responsibility. He must expose to his European audience the naked reality of the relationship between Europe and the third world. He has to show to his European reader that, to paraphrase Brecht, the water he drinks is often taken from the mouths of the thirsty in the third world, and the food he eats is snatched from the mouths of the hungry in Asia, Africa and South America.

But the responsibility also belongs to the writer from the third world. From Kenya to South Korea to South America the third world is ringed round by U.S. nuclear and conventional military bases. The United States supports the most repressive regimes in the third world. Uncle Sam sits on the backs of millions in the third world and loudly calls for stability. The third world writer must be on the side of the struggles of those sat upon.

Now I cannot remember in detail how Sindbad solved his predicament but I think he eventually managed to give the old man of the sea some intoxicating drink and the man slid off Sindbad's back. But would his solution been so simple if the old man of the sea had been armed with nuclear weaponry? Probably not, but the necessity to struggle and make the old man get off his back would not have been diminished by his knowledge of the destructive might of his oppressor.

Literature provides us with images of the world in which we live. Through these images, it shapes our consciousness to look at the world in a certain way. Our propensity to action or inaction or to a certain kind of action or inaction can be profoundly affected by the way we look at the world.

Writing for peace should at the very least mean raising human consciousness to an uncompromising hatred of all exploitative parasitic relations between nations and between peoples within each nation. In our world today, this would mean continued exposure and opposition to imperialism currently led by the U.S. "Get off our back!" should be the unanimous cry of all the democratic forces of peace. For we must all struggle for a world in which one's cleanliness is not dependent on another's dirt, one's health on another's ill-health, and one's welfare on another's misery.

Peace is only possible in a world in which the condition of the development of any one nation is the development of all.

---

*This paper was given at The International Literature Conference in Cologne, West Germany, in August 1982.

National Identity and
Imperialist Domination:

The Crisis of Culture in Africa Today*

The crisis of culture in Africa (and the developing world) has too often been seen in terms of a conflict between tradition and modernity; the rural and the urban; and the clash of values consequently engendered by that dichotomy. In this schema, the urban (industry, technology, electronics, etc.) is identified with modernity; the rural (subsistence agriculture, economic backwardness, etc.) with tradition. But ironically the same modernity is supposed to evoke images of fast changes, instability, human isolation while tradition evokes contrary images of peace, stability, and communal existence. Rampant urbanization and industrialization are seen as destroying a harmony of values embodied in tradition whose repository is the rural community. Thus the false glitter of the electronic culture is seen as luring an unwary youth away from the stability of communal life in a rural village into the chaos and loneliness of life in the big city.

It is all there in written literature. The peasant who follows the mirage of prosperity and happiness in the big city only to find the opposite is a familiar character in many a novel from the developing world. What often is not stated is that such a character is actually escaping from the hell of rural poverty and misery into the hades of urban poverty and misery, in both cases brought about by ruthless exploitation, internal and external. But even where this is stated, the schema of rural/urban dichotomy as the basis of analysis of the problems of culture in developing countries remains, and the crisis of culture is still seen in terms of a conflict between tradition and modernity.

Two misleading assumptions underlie the schema.

Firstly, modern industry, science and technology are seen as being in opposition to tradition and peasant cultures. The destruction of tradition or aspects of tradition and peasant culture is seen as necessarily evil. Within this false schema the beauty of rural culture rests on a foundation of poverty and abject want. But in fact modern science and technology, if organized, owned and controlled differently, could make possible a total economic transformation of the countryside and the construction of a whole people's culture on a structure of prosperity instead of on that of backwardness. Moreover, far from destroying tradition, modern technology (e.g. video, cinema, television, radio) should make it possible to actually reclaim the positive aspects of tradition and peasant cultures which are withering away under the pressures of the economic exploitation. Africa, for instance, has a rich tradition of oral literature. The narrative was often accompanied by mime and song. With video, film and television, it is now possible to reclaim this tradition through an integration of the visual image (e.g. animated cartoons), the voice and the music. The same is true in theater. African peasant theater relied heavily on song, dance and mime, and these can now be permanently captured on the screen. Thus not only is it possible to use modern science and technology to democratize access to this heritage—more people can be told the tale at the same time—but even more crucial, it is possible to use it to integrate the cultures of the different nationalities within the geographic state into a national whole. Through video, T.V. or cinema, the tales from the different nationalities become mutually accessible and comprehensible.

The second misleading assumption is that the rural and the urban are two self-contained islands and a character from one to the other is actually walking across two unlinked entities. But in fact the two are a creation of each other. The urban is a creation of the rural as much as the rural is a creation of the urban. The peasants had to be alienated from the soil and be driven into towns, that is, they had to be proletarianized before the modern city could be born. But where under feudal and semifeudal systems the town was under the sway of the countryside, the modern city which emerged with capitalism, the city of gold, became the master of the rural out of which it had been born and bred. Marx and Engels wrote of 19th century Europe:

> The bourgeoisie has subjected the country to the rule of the towns. It has
> created enormous cities, has greatly increased the urban population as
> compared with the rural, and has thus rescued a considerable part of the
> population from the idiocy of rural life. Just as it has made the country de-

pendent upon towns, so it has made barbarian and semibarbarian countries dependent on the civilized ones, nations of peasants on nations of
bourgeoisie, the East on the West.

With the evolution of capitalism into the higher stage of imperialism,
the rural and urban sectors of "the nations of peasants" became even
more subjected to the rule of "the nations of bourgeoisie," and with what
results? The subject nations—that is the majority of the population—
were reduced to the idiocy of both urban and rural life.

This economic and political subjection of "the nations of peasants" to
"the nations of bourgeoisie" is the heart of the matter when discussing
cultural problems of the developing countries. For economic and political
dependence are bound to be reflected in culture.

But by posing the problems of culture in the developing world in terms
of a conflict between the rural and the urban, thus concentrating on
secondary contradictions, the real issues behind the crisis are avoided.
What are the real forces behind modernity and tradition, the urban and
the rural? Viewed in a historical perspective, the whole problem (modernity, tradition, rural, urban, etc.) brings us face to face with the inescapable
fact: the all encompassing impact of imperialism on third world peoples
and the national struggles which that very impact has generated.

The developing world, with its economic, political and cultural backwardness, its massive poverty, illiteracy and disease, is a creation of imperialism in its colonial and neocolonial stages. The developing world can
in fact be defined as all those countries in Asia, Africa and Latin America
which have been underdeveloped by imperialism, those countries whose
economy, politics and culture have been and continue to be dominated
by Western imperialist nations, in essence meaning the subjection of the
whole population of the dominated countries to the ruling bourgeois
classes of the dominating nations. Marx and Engels wrote:

> The bourgeoisie by the rapid development of all instruments of production,
> by the immensely facilitated means of communication, draws all, even the
> most barbarian, nations into civilization. The cheap prices of its com-
> modities are the heavy artillery with which it batters down all Chinese
> walls, with which it forces the barbarians intensely obstinate hatred of
> foreigners to capitulate. It compels all nations, on pain of extinction to
> adopt the bourgeois mode of production; it compels them to introduce
> what it calls civilization into the midst, i.e. to become bourgeois
> themselves. In a word, it creates a world after its own image.

A world after its own image: this it tried to achieve not only through
economic exploitation and political subjugation but more importantly,
through cultural domination. Economic and political control have never
been possible without a mental control. Thus the robbery of a peoples'
wealth was accompanied by a repressive political colonial rule enforced
by the gun and the boot and also a programmed attempt to destroy peo-

ple's dances, songs, literature, religions, languages, while imposing the conqueror's languages, literature, education and religion.

The colonial system could not of course hold cultural captive the entire population. That would have been an achievement unparalleled in history. But they had an achievement of a sort which is now proving so fatal to real development in Africa. They created a colonial elite. In his introduction to Frantz Fanon's classic, *The Wretched of the Earth*, Jean-Paul Sartre has aptly and ably described the process of creating a colonial elite in the image of the Western bourgeois:

> They picked out promising adolescents; they branded them, as with red-hot iron, with the principles of Western culture; they stuffed their mouths full of high-sounding phrases, grand glutinous words that stuck to their teeth. After a short stay in the mother country they were sent home, whitewashed. These walking lies had nothing to say to their brothers; they only echoed. From Paris, from London, from Amsterdam we would utter the words "Parthenon! Brotherhood!" and somewhere in Asia or Africa lips would open ". . . thenon! . . . therhood!"

This elite saw the world, they perceived themselves and the possibilities opened out to them, with glasses "Made in Europe" and which were now permanently glued to their eyes.

But the process created its opposite: the economic, political and cultural struggle for national independence and total liberation. This resulted in some sort of independence with the elite manufactured in Europe a la Sartre's description inheriting the state with one dictum signed at the end of Constitutional Conferences: don't change the colonial economic structures of dependence! On the cultural level, in the colonies and neocolonies there grew two cultures in mortal conflict: foreign imperialist; national and patriotic. And so, out of the different nationalities often inhabiting one geographic state, there emerged a people's literature, music, dance, theater, art in fierce struggle against foreign imperialist literature, music, dance, theater, art imposed on colonies, semicolonies, and neocolonies. Thus the major contradiction in the third world is between national identity and imperialist domination.

This to me is still the real and fundamental conflict of cultures: viz, a national patriotic culture arising out of and getting its character from the struggle against imperialism. Other contradictions, between the urban and the rural, the modern and the traditional, and between the different nationalities are secondary and they can only be properly appreciated within the context of the larger basic contradiction.

In this conflict, the national tries to find roots in the traditions mostly kept alive by the peasantry in the forms of their songs, poems, theater and dances. The foreign imperialist culture tries to build strongholds in the cities where it parades itself as modernity and progress. Thus this crucial struggle between the national and foreign is deliberately made to appear as a conflict between the rural and the urban or between tradition and modernity.

This is not an accident. The impoverished exploited peasantry with its oral heritage lives in the countryside. But the native bourgeoisie through whom imperialism works resides in the city. It controls the state instruments of coercion, persuasion and propaganda. In their state theaters, cinemas, television and radio stations, they mostly allow only reactionary foreign programs. They champion the cause of imperialism which they present as "modern and national" while in the countryside they pay lip service to peasant cultures by championing irrelevant traditionalism emptied of all meaningful dynamic content, a petrified museum culture for the amusement of state guests and tourists.

But even in these towns and cities, new cultures are emerging out of that struggle for total liberation from imperialism. This can be clearly seen in the poetry and songs and theatre among workers in the urban areas of the developing world. It is a fighting culture, and though fusing different elements, it is in basic harmony with the resistance culture of the countryside. The urban and the rural struggles are actually in basic harmony in their opposition to exploitation and domination by an alliance of a servile native ruling class and imperialism. Thus the worker and the peasant are the basis and creators of truly modern cultures in the developing world because all through the colonial and neocolonial stages they have resisted being branded with the red-hot irons of Western bourgeois values and outlook. These worker/peasant cultures are national in character and are in basic conflict with all forms of foreign domination.

This real conflict of cultures in Africa between imperialism and resistance is rapidly moving toward a crisis. This is because so many of the ruling regimes in the developing world are committed to both nurturing, promoting and encouraging foreign reactionary cultures while at the same time actively suppressing any genuine progressive national initiatives.

Kenya is a case in point. It got flag independence in 1963, a concession, but nevertheless a result of 60 years of the Kenyan people's protracted political struggle whose highest peak was the Mau Mau armed resistance against the British. The Kenyan people's struggle has taken many forms, but the cultural has always been dominant. Thus during the colonial era of national resistance, poetry, theater, dance and songs developed in opposition to the settler white culture of cheap novels, religion of slavery, brothels, prostitution, and theater imported from London. The settler colonial regime retaliated by banning Kenya People's theater, songs and dances, often jailing and detaining artists who refused to comply. Thus in the thirties the Muthirigu dance/drama movement was banned and many of the composers, dancers and poets imprisoned. The same was true in the fifties when many Mau Mau writers, publishers, poets, singers were sent to prisons and detention camps. At the same time, the settler colonial regime tried to nurture a procolonial theater, dance, song and poetry among Kenyans and especially through the school system. English language and the literature, philosophy, culture, and values it carried was elevated to the skies. African languages and the literature and philosophy they carried were brutally suppressed.

Today the situation has not changed. The ruling authorities are in ecstacy and frenzy when promoting foreign-language theater and music. English is still the official language and is the language of education from primary schools to university. African languages are not promoted. To the Kenyan authorities, Kenyan languages are only fit to carry Christian messages through religious hymns and biblical homilies on the national radio system and in churches every Sunday.

At the Kenya National Theater, foreigners, especially if they happen to be British or American, are free to put on any theatrical shows, trite, ridiculous and even racist. And this foreign theater will find patronage among very highly placed Africans. The other day, in May 1982, we witnessed a very interesting spectacle of highly placed Kenyans all trooping to the Kenyan National Theater to see the ballet version of *Alice in Wonderland*. Certainly no foreign play or any play by foreign European groups has ever been stopped by the Kenyan authorities.

But recently the authorities went even further, certainly beyond ordinary comprehension. They bought *Flame Trees of Thika*, a film in seven episodes based on Elspeth Huxley's book of the same title, and showed it on Kenya national television. Elspeth Huxley was a spokeswoman of the British colonial settler regime. *Flame Trees of Thika* treats her childhood in the Kenya of the twenties and thirties, a time when the settler regime was brutally planting roots in the labor of Kenyan workers, whose land they had already taken by holy guile and brutal force. The book and the film portray Kenyans as dumb creatures, part and parcel of the animal and natural landscape. It is very racist and understandably many Kenyans were outraged by the film and they wrote many letters of protest. One letter in *The Daily Nation* of April 19 summed up the national outrage by describing the episode as stinking. But all the seven episodes were shown despite the national outcry.

There is basically nothing wrong in Elspeth Huxley portraying reality from her settler's colonial point of view. There is even nothing wrong in having that view shown.

But the state patronage of colonial culture is a big contrast to the brutal suppression of Kenyan People's cultural initiatives. In 1977 for instance the peasants and workers from Kamiriithu Community Educational and Cultural Center, Limuru, built a huge open air theater in their village and put on a play *Ngaahika Ndeenda (I Will Marry When I Want)* to an acclaim by thousands. But the Kenyan authorities stepped in and stopped the show. Early in 1982, the same group put on another play, *Maitu Njugira (Mother Sing For Me)* and once again the authorities refused to issue a license for a public performance. Instead the group was hounded out of the Kenya National Theater and University premises.

Maitu Njugira is set in the twenties and thirties and treats the same period as that covered by Huxley's *Flame Trees of Thika*. The musical depicted the struggle of Kenyan workers against the very repressive colonial labor laws including the 1915 labor registration act which came into effect in 1919 and which required workers to carry passes in metal containers hanging from their necks.

You would think that every Kenyan would be very happy about this. But no. A Kenyan play showing that Kenyans were not dumb creatures, at the sole mercy of the settler, was hounded out of the Kenyan National Theater. Yet a film showing that Kenyans had no capacity for resistance, that they were part and parcel of the wilderness, could be given prime time on television for several weeks. National facilities and state money could be used in April and May 1982 to facilitate the showing of *Flame Trees of Thika* but in February and May, a musical acted by ordinary folk could not be allowed into the national premises. The authorities went even further. Three truckloads of armed policemen were later rushed to Kamiriithu Center and razed the whole open air theater to the ground. Kamiriithu Community Educational and Cultural Center's license was revoked and all drama activities in the village banned. The poor peasants had no rights to enjoy theater even in their own backyards.

Unfortunately, the closure of Kamiriithu Community Educational and Cultural Center and the banning of all theater activities by the peasants and workers of the village is not an isolated event in the cultural life of Kenya. It is part of a trend; it is part of a programed attempt by the authorities at organized repression of thought. In January, *Muntu* by Joe de Graft, performed by the Literature Department of Kenyatta University College, was suspended. *Muntu* shows the historical emergence of neocolonies in Africa and had originally been commissioned by the All-Africa Conference of Churches. Another play, *Kilio (The Cry)*, written and produced by Nairobi school and a winning play at the Kenya School Drama Festival at Kakamega, was refused performance at the University of Nairobi. Five lecturers at the Kenyatta University College and one from Nairobi University have been arrested and are awaiting detention or trial. One of the lecturers, Amin Mazrui, a linguist, is also the author of *Kilio cha Haki (Cry for Justice)*. Students now have to swear loyalty, actually have to be screened for loyalty, before they can be admitted to university. The government will soon be choosing the texts to be used in schools, especially texts for literature. Thus the students will only be reading that which the government of the day wants them to read and study and not necessarily what's required by the demands of their academic discipline and subject matter.

What's happening in Kenya, a programed repression of people's cultural initiative and thought, is of course very extreme, but it may not be that fundamentally different from what's happening in a number of developing countries; i.e. a servile worship of what is foreign and antinational and an active suppression of what's genuinely national and progressive.

The testimony now comes from Latin America but it could as well come from Asia: South Korea and the Philippines, for instance. But let me quote from an interview with Jorge Musto, published in *Index on Censorship*, Vol. 11, No. 1, February 1982. Jorge Musto is an Uruguayan novelist and he was asked by *Index* "Can you tell us something about the repression launched against culture when the military took power in 1973?" He responded:

> First of all I think the repression was so effective because, unfortunately, it was intelligent. It was carried out gradually, bit by bit, without creating too many enemies at once. Different sectors of society were attacked one after the other according to a hierarchy of real or supposed dangers worked out by the strategists of repression. First of all the armed opposition was dealt with, then parliament and the political parties—starting with the left and eventually working through to the traditional right as well—then trade unions and the press. By the time they got round to culture there were very few activities in the country which remained untouched. Education, perhaps, but I have the idea that this was hit together with culture. Cultural activity at that time was of very high quality. Apart from theater, book publishers were flourishing, the press generally speaking expressed a wide range of opinion, there were several cine-clubs. All in all, cultural activity at every level was extremely fluid and fertile. Meanwhile the University of Montevideo had become an open forum for debate, where the social and cultural concerns of the moment were discussed and projected beyond its own cloisters. All this was to all intents and purposes wiped out by such methods as torture, detention and exile. University teachers and those involved in the cultural field were almost without exception firm opponents of the regime which was attempting to impose itself at that time—the run-up to the final takeover by the military. In political terms, such people were considered dangerous enemies. So they were repressed.

Musto's testament gives one strange sensations: he could have been talking, word for word, on what has happened on countless occasions in different parts of Asia and Africa.

This repression by corrupt regimes in places like Uruguay and Kenya is being carried out in the name of Western civilization and those principles of "Western culture" red-hot-iron-branded on the minds of the neoslaves. There is a logic to this. Aid and investment from the West are equated with Western civilization. The regimes are incapable of conceiving development outside the vicious cycle of aid, investment, dependency and more aid, investment and dependency. Stability must be maintained at every human cost: the countries must be kept safe for Western profit seekers. This inability to bring about real change in the inherited colonial structures because of blinkered visions, congenital corruption and utter inefficiency, makes them more and more isolated from the people. Result: democracy becomes a luxury: there is too much democracy in this country, they proclaim unashamedly, looking, for their image of authority, to the golden era of colonialism when the settler exploited labor and imposed his will and ruled with guns, sjamboks and nailed boots. Are they not the modern "settler" albeit with black skins, at least in the case of Africa? The fact is that these repressive regimes are able to survive against a hostile and restive population because of the support they get from their Western donors. Even where repression has become so naked that private investment becomes nervous and manifestly shy of accepting the open-armed invitation, the regimes can hobble on because of infusion of aid from their "traditional" friends. The result of this is a virtual mortgage of the future of those countries to the donors: such aid has also a larger purpose: to tie up the hands of any future regimes which are bound to honor the international commitments of their predecessors. In time aid and grants may seem safer and cheaper than private investments, and so the cycle of instability, repression, autocracy, becomes guaranteed and underwritten by aid, grants and other donations. These regimes with endless access to arsenals of repression and all sorts of military toys in the end come to conceive of themselves as no more than hired policemen of Western interests and they will even sulk and act hurt when criticized by their "friends" for doing away with such luxuries as multiparty systems, freedoms of assembly and expression, rights to seek, receive and impart information and ideas, rights to a cultural life independent of government manipulation. Why should a people's culture stand in the way of a hired policeman and his duties to Christianity and Western civilization? Christianity and Western civilization—what countless crimes have been done in thy name!

It could be a matter for despair. But, at the same time, the contrary process is intensifying too. All over the third world people are more and more realizing that no country can consider itself free for as long as its economy and culture are dominated by foreigners. Hence alongside political and economic struggles lies a cultural struggle exemplified by the Kamiriithus of the developing world. The struggle for national identity through a national economy and an independent political line in national and international affairs comes face to face with the brutal realities of imperialist domination through a ruling elite that has completely internalized slave values. But that very national identity is getting its shape and character from that struggle. The two, national identity through mass struggles, and imperialist domination through westernized corrupt regimes, are heading toward the final collision.

This is what has brought Africa and the rest of the developing world to its present crisis point, a situation that often makes some of our detractors raise their hands in horror and declare that Africa is falling apart, conveniently forgetting that at the root of all our problems is still the imperialist domination of our economic, political and cultural life.

It is quite clear, to me at least, that a prerequisite of Africa's cultural development is a continued intensified struggle for its complete economic and political liberation from all vestiges of imperialism. This also means a continued intensified struggle against the comprador ruling class through whom imperialist interests continue to dominate the lives of millions of peasants and workers of the developing world.

A new world economic and political order would mean a new world cultural order and this would see the flowering of a great modern culture in Africa and the rest of the developing world, a culture that has roots in the dynamic progressive aspects of a national tradition while remaining open to the progressive and humanist cultural elements all over the world.

---

*This is a revised version of a paper I wrote for UNESCO and which appeared in UNESCO Courier under the title: *National Identity and Foreign Domination*. This revised version was first publicly delivered as a speech to the Royal Commonwealth Society and the Royal African Society in London, June 10, 1982 and to Oxford University African Society on June 11, 1982, under the title: *The Crisis of Culture in Africa*. I have subsequently read it at the Univesities of Gothenburg, Lund, Uppsala, Umea and Stockholm in Sweden, September 1982.

Education for a National Culture*

I feel it slightly presumptuous on my part to stand here, in Zimbabwe, and talk about education and culture. For a people who have entered the highest phase of political struggle, that is the phase of armed struggle, against foreign rule and oppression, have already laid firm educational foundations for a national patriotic culture. For it's both an act of education and an educational process to struggle to seize back the right and the initiative to make one's own history and hence culture which is a product and a reflection of that history. Guinea-Bissau's Amilcar Cabral has rightly said that national liberation is necessarily an act of culture, and the liberation movement "the organized political expression of the struggling people's culture."

So let me start by congratulating the heroic people of Zimbabwe for their successful armed struggle against the colonial stage of imperialism. I talk of the colonial stage because imperialism has in fact two stages: colonial and neocolonial. The failure, or the deliberate refusal to recognize this and hence the pitfalls into which a successful anticolonial struggle can fall is already costing many an African country dear in terms of economic misery—turning beggary and charity into national institutions.

By organizing a conference imbued with the spirit and desire for a structural social transformation as outlined in the letter of invitation from the Minister for Education, the people of Zimbabwe, I take it, have already seen the possibilities and hence the dangers of neocolonialism—what Kwame Nkrumah once described as the last stage of imperialism.

Education and culture can play a decisive role in the social transformation so vital and necessary for a victory over the neocolonial stage of imperialism.

But what education and what culture? What's the relationship between

87

the two? And what have these got to do with economic, political and social transformation of society?

Education is the process of integrating the youth into the entire system of social production, exchange and distribution of what we eat, wear and shelter under, the whole system of organizing the wealth of a given country. It does so (1) by imparting knowledge about the two basic relations on which the entire society including its culture is erected: i.e. the relations between man and nature and relations between man and man, and (2) by imparting a certain outlook or attitude to the two relations. Now the world outlook of a people is embodied in their moral, aesthetic and ethical values which are in turn embodied in their culture. Their culture is itself a product and a reflection of the history built on the two relations with nature and with other men. Thus education is part of culture and culture is part of education. They run into each other, and one way of looking at education is as a process of integrating a people into the dominant culture of that community.

Let me illustrate this by going over a familiar ground.

Man like animals is part of nature. But unlike animals he produces his means of life: what he eats, wears and shelters under. His labor power acting on nature produces his food, clothing, shelter, and other needs to meet other needs. His labor power acting on natural resources generates wealth. His labor power is made more powerful by the use of tools, that is instruments of labor, from the simplest sharpened stone to the most complicated machinery; by his skills and ability to utilize the tools, i.e. technology; and by his cooperation with other men in his struggle to wrest a living from nature.

The relations between man and nature are characterized by both harmony and conflict: harmony because, being part of nature, whatever man does is a manifestation of nature; and conflict because he must detach himself from nature, act on it, change it, turn it into a slave, compel it to meet his needs. Nature itself is not passive and often acts hostile to man. Struggle is the essence of man's relations with nature.

But in struggling with nature, man enters into relations with other men in two ways. He must cooperate with others, through division of labor, to face hostile nature. When we talk of human labor power over nature, we are talking of cooperative human labor. Thus the production of wealth is a social act, the result of many hands. Once he has wrestled with nature and has compelled it to yield, he now must share out the fruits, the products, the wealth resulting from that cooperative struggle with nature. The relations between man and man are characterized by both harmony and conflict: harmony or cooperation when he joins with others to face nature, and conflict when it comes to sharing that which their combined labor-power has wrested from nature. Struggle is the essence of man's relations with man, since even in production he will try to occupy a place that gives him an advantageous position in the exchange and distribution of their common wealth. For instance, those who, in the evolution of a society, come to own the means of production (the tools of labor, natural resources and even human labor power itself) control the distribution of the common or social wealth.

The relations that men enter into with one another in the production of wealth through the productive forces are relations of production and constitute the economic structure of that community. Thus the two relations or rather the two struggles (with nature and with other men) are the foundation of any society and they are linked together by human labor power in production. It is first an economic community.

But in the process of the economic evolution of that community, they work out rules that govern and regulate their economic life: i.e. their relations with nature and with one another over both production and the sharing of the social product. They even evolve machinery for enforcing the rules. Thus the economic community evolves into a political community with often a form of state (the military, the police, the judges with law courts and prisons) for enforcing the rules governing and regulating their economic life. So our community has also a political life; it is a political community.

In the process of their economic and political life, the community develops a way of life often seemingly unique to that society. They evolve language, song, dance, literature, religion, theater, art, architecure, and an education system that transmits all those plus a knowledge of the history and the geography of their territory of habitation from one generation to the next. Thus our economic and political community evolves a cultural life expressed in their languages, art, architecture, dance, song, theater, literature, and their educational system. It is a community of culture, linked together by a shared way of life.

A people's culture is the carrier of the values evolved by that community in the course of their economic and political life. By values I mean their conception of what's right and wrong (moral values); what's good and bad (ethical values); and what's ugly and beautiful (aesthetic values).

The values they hold are the basis of that community's consciousness, the basis of their world outlook, the basis of their collective and individual image of self, that is the selfhood of that community, their identity as a people who look at themselves and their relationships to the universe in a certain way.

This is not a mechanical process, occurring in neat steps and springs with the economic structure giving rise to political and other institutions and these in turn giving rise to culture, values, consciousness and identity in that order. The processes are often evolving more or less simultaneously with one process generating several others at the same time. Nor is it all a one-way traffic with economic life flowing into political and cultural life. It's a dialectical process. How people look at themselves affects the way they look at their values which in turn affects the way they look at their culture, at their political and economic life and ultimately at their relations with nature. It's a complex process with things acting on each other to produce what we call society.

What's the role of education in that scheme? Ideally, education should give people the knowledge about the world in which they live: how the world shapes them and how they shape the world. Education should transmit a culture that inculcates in the people a consciousness that man through his labor power is the creator of his social environment and that in the same way that man acts on nature and changes it, he can also act on his social environment and change it and in the process change himself. Previously nature used to confront man as a hostile incomprehensible force until he was able to understand its hidden laws (e.g. gravity) and hence overcame it and turned it into a servant. Today under capitalism man's social environment confronts him as a hostile force. When he finally understands its hidden laws, he'll overcome it, transcend it, and so create a new world for a new man, where both the natural and social environment are servants of man. Education should give people the confidence that they can in fact create a new heaven on this earth.

But what education are we talking about? Depending on who is wielding the weapon, education far from being a means of illuminating reality can be used as a means of masking reality to mystify the relations between man and nature and between man and man. In his novel, *Hard Times*, Dickens has very neatly demonstrated how education can be used to mystify and often obscure reality. The setting is in a school run by a Mr. Thomas Grandgrind in an industrial town. In the school, people are to be taught nothing but facts so as to eliminate forever the habit of wondering about "human nature, human passions, human hopes and fears, and struggles, defeats, the cares and sorrows, the lives and deaths of common men and women!" In the school are two characters, Sissy Jupe, a girl who has lived among horses all her life because her father works in a circus. Then there's Blitzer, a boy who has never once seen a horse in his life. In the class, Thomas Grandgrind suddenly asks Sissy Jupe, the girl, to give a definition of a horse, and the girl is thrown into the greatest alarm by this sudden demand and she cannot define a horse. Thomas Grandgrind, after announcing that the girl is unable to define a horse, "One of the commonest of animals," now turns to Blitzer, the boy who has never lived among horses.

"Blitzer," says Thomas Grandgrind, "Your definition of a horse."

The boy stands up and with great bravado spews out the definition of a horse learnt from books.

"Quadruped. Graminivorous. Forty teeth, namely twenty-four grinders, four eye-teeth, and twelve incisive. Sheds coat in the spring; in marshy countries, sheds hoofs, too. Hoofs hard, but requiring to be shod with iron. Age known by marks in mouth."

The teacher now turns to the girl and says: "Now . . . you know what a horse is!"

But in reality, in practice, it's the girl, Sissy Jupe, who knows all about horses, and it's the boy, Blitzer, who does not. Jupe, the girl, knows the reality of a horse for she has touched one, fed it, rode on it, and has lived among them. Blitzer, the boy, only knows a horse in words, as a mental abstraction. Here education is being used to mystify and obscure reality.

Why is this? If we go back to our hypothetical human community or society we shall find that the economic structure is at the same time a class structure with some people owning the means of production and hence the productive forces (human labor power, the instruments of labor, raw materials and the natural resources) while others do not own the means. In other words, in the process of people acting on nature to produce their means of life, they come to stand in different positions in the production process. The relations of production, the relations between man and man and between man and the forces of production (labor plus tools of labor and objects of labor), is not one of equality, but often one of the exploiter and the exploited, the oppressor and the oppressed. In a slave society, the slave-owner owns everything; in a feudal society, the nobility owns the land and the peasants rent it from them. In a capitalist society, the owner of capital owns all the means of production and the worker has only his labor power. Yet it's the slave, the peasant, the worker who does all the production, who creates the wealth of that society, and yet is not able to control the disposal of that which his sweat has generated. Since in such societies, the economic structure is at the same time a class structure, all the institutions, political and cultural, will bear the stamp of this or that class. Education and culture will reflect these class cleavages at the economic foundation of that society. Education and culture are in fact class education and culture.

Thus in a class structured society, or in a situation where one nation or race or class is dominated by another, there can never be any neutral education transmitting a neutral culture. For the oppressing class or nation or race, education becomes an instrument of suppression, that is an instrument for the conservation of the prevailing social order; and for the struggling class, race or nation, it becomes an instrument of liberation, that is, an instrument for the social transformation of the status quo. In such a society, there are in fact two types of education in mortal struggle, transmitting two opposed types of culture and hence two opposed consciousnesses or world outlooks or ideologies.

Let me illustrate this. *A* is sitting on *B*. *A* is carried, fed and clothed by *B*. What kind of education will *A* want *B* to get? In other words, education for what kind of culture and ideologized consciousness? *A* will want to educate *B* to obscure the fact that it is *B* who is carrying, feeding and clothing *A*. *A* will want *B* to learn the philosophy which says the world does not change. *A* will want to teach *B* the religion which tells him that the present situation is divinely willed and nothing can be done about it, or that *B* is in the present plight because he has sinned, or that *B* should endure his lot because in heaven he will get plenty. Religion, any religion, is very useful to *A* for it teaches that the situation in which *A* is sitting on *B* is not brought about by man; it is not historical: on the contrary, it's a natural law of the universe, sanctioned by God. *A* will want *B* to believe that he, *B*, has no culture or his culture is inferior. *A* will then want *B* to imbibe a culture that inculcates in him values of self-doubt, self-denigration, in a word, a slave consciousness.

He will now look up to *A's* superior culture. In short, *A* will want *B* to have the education which on one hand will deny him real knowledge about the status quo of an *A* sitting on a *B* or the historical origins of a situation where *A* is stting on *B*; and on the other, impart a culture embodying values of slavery, a slave consciousness or world outlook. This will make *B* subservient. For *A* wants *B* not only to be a slave but to accept that his fate or destiny is to be a slave.

B on the other hand will want that philosophy that teaches that everything changes, that change is inherent in nature and human society. He will embrace that religion which preaches that the system of some people sitting on others is against the law of God. *B* may want to reevaluate his past and he will discover that he was not always a slave, carrying, feeding and clothing *A*. Thus he will embrace that education that shows him quite clearly that his present plight is historical and not natural, that it has been brought about by man and so can be changed by man. *B* will embrace that culture which inculcates in him values of self-confidence and pride in self, values which give him courage and faith that he can do something about his present plight, in short *B* will want that education which not only gives knowledge about his plight, but a liberated consciousness, a consciousness urging him to fight for freedom.

Now it is possible that *A* and *B* are not necessarily conscious of the type of education and culture and world outlook they want. But the fact remains that there is an education system which imparts a culture embodying a consciousness corresponding to the objective position of *A*, and another corresponding to the objective position of *B*. The two types of education, culture and world outlook, are in mortal struggle for *A* is trying to make *B* embrace a slave consciousness so that he, *A*, can exploit and oppress in peace. But *B* is also struggling to evolve an education that imparts a culture that frees him from the intended slave consciousness so he can with confidence overturn *A* and be free to now carry, feed and clothe himself.

We can see the situation of *A* and *B* more concretely if we look at education and culture under imperialism in its colonial and neocolonial stages.

Colonialism broadly speaking is that situation in which the ruling class of one nation or country imposes its rule and hegemony over another nation and country and subjugates and suppresses all the other classes of the colonized country. The aim is the control of the productive forces of the colonized country and hence the wealth produced by the colonized peoples. But colonialism finds that economic control is impossible without a political control, so after a successful military conquest and occupation of the country, colonialism imposes political control either directly through a white settler presence as in Kenya, Zimbabwe, Algeria or through a white administration but one working indirectly through feudal elements and missionary products as in Uganda, Ghana and Nigeria.

Even then, colonialism finds that economic and political control are incomplete without cultural and hence ideological control. So colonialism imposes an education system which denies the colonized real knowledge about the wealth produced in the land while at the same time imparting a culture embodying a slave-consciousness.

Thus the colonized are taught that they have no history, meaning they have never acted on nature and changed it. Their history, they are told, started with the arrival of the whites carrying banners of a Christian civilization. Before colonialism, wrote Professor Trevor-Roper of Oxford University in 1960, there was only darkness in Africa and as darkness was no subject for history, Africa had therefore no history prior to colonial conquest. A land of darkness and perpetual childhood, cried Hegel. Where there was clear evidence of advanced civilizations as in Ethiopia and Egypt, then arguments were brought to show or prove that these people were not Africans. (cf: Greece is generally recognized as the cradle of European civilization. But nobody tries to prove, argue or claim that the Greeks were not really Europeans!) Where there was evidence of a very highly developed material culture with an architecture often superior to that of Europe of the same period as in Zimbabwe and East Africa, then arguments about a previous white or Arab presence, despite lack of historical evidence, are advanced to explain away such achievements. Denying that people had a history has one aim: to show that the colonized like animals had merely adapted themselves to nature and had made no attempt to put a human stamp on their natural environment. Hence they were really savages!

Education for a National Culture

The colonial education system denies that the colonized have real human languages. These are described as vernaculars meaning the languages of slaves or merely barbaric tongues.So the children of the colonized are punished and ridiculed whenever they are caught speaking their mother's language, and rewarded when they speak the language of the master, French, English, Portuguese or Italian as the case may be. This had one aim: to make a child despise his language, hence the values carried by that language, and by implication despise himself and the people who spoke a language which now was the cause of his daily humiliation and corporal punishment. By the same token he will admire the language of the conqueror, and hence the values carried by that language and the people who evolved the language of his daily reward and praise.

But these values are reinforced by Christianity, particularly the version brought by missionaries. To the European colonizer the African has no religion, he knows not God. He is superstitious, and worships idols and several Gods. There is only one God, though he has a Son, begotten by the Holy Spirit. This God is white: his angels are white; and when the saved finally go to heaven, they will wear white robes of purity. But the devil is black; his angels are black; sin itself is black; and when the sinful finally go to Hell, they'll be burnt to black charcoal. Is it surprising that the African converts sing in pleading terror: Wash me Redeemer and I shall be whiter than snow? Is it any wonder that African converts wear white robes of virgin purity during their white wedding? And is it any wonder that African women often buy red, blond or brunette wigs to hide their black hair? And is it any wonder that African women and men will apply *Ambi* and other skinwhitening creams to lighten their dark skins? Whiteness becomes a Christian virtue as in Smith's Rhodesia and Botha's South Africa.

Christianity even denies that the African has a right to his name. A name is a simple symbol of identity. The African convert will discard his African name and give himself such good Christian names as Smith, Welensky, Verwoerd, Robert, James,Julius, Ironmonger,Winterbottom, Elizabeth, Mary, Margaret, Summer and Winter! He does not realize that this business of getting new names has roots in slavery where the slave dealer branded the slave with his own mark and gave him his name so that he would forever be known as that master's property.

The same story is true in art, dance, music, drama and literature. The Good African in European fiction on Africa is he who collaborates with colonialism. The bad native is he who rejects colonial occupation and wants to assert himself and struggle to get back the stolen wealth. Thus in a book called *King Solomon's Mines* by Rider Haggard, the blacks like Gagool who want to prevent the foreigners from exploiting the country's natural assets like gold and diamonds are painted in most revolting terms. Such books are even translated into African languages like Kiswahili and Shona by colonial Literature Bureaux so the African can clearly understand the message of slavery. The reader's emotions are guided in such a way that he cannot possibly identify with the patriots. But the traitors are described in positive terms of courage, honesty, diligence and intelligence. But it is courage, honesty, diligence and intelligence in selling fellow Africans to colonialist Europeans. Even in books which do not delineate the African character in terms of animals and landscape, that is, in books by liberal Europeans, the African character held for admiration and presented as worthy of emulation is the non-violent, spineless type, the type who turns the other cheek, the right cheek once the left cheek has been hit by a racist colonialist whitey. Such for instance is Rev. Stephen Kumalo in Alan Paton's poisonous novel *Cry the Beloved Country* or Johnson in Joyce Cary's *Mr. Johnson*. Incidentally even the most racist of white characters in *Cry the Beloved Country* would be quite happy to have a Bishop Stephen Kumalo for a prime minister!

In art, illustrating books on Africa written by intellectuals of colonialism, the European colonizer occupies the central stage of action and drama with light radiating outwards from him. The African native is in the background and merges with darkness and natural scenery at the outer edges of the action. When the Makerere School of Fine Art was started in the sixties, the European lecturers used to import clay from Europe. Ugandan soil was not good enough for art, even though the students were all Africans.

The sum total of this type of education in the teaching of geography (rocks and rivers and mountains of Europe first); history (Africa was discovered by Europe; Africa is a continuation of Europe), art, literature, theater, is to socialize the African youth into a culture embodying values and hence a consciousness and world outlook which on the one hand is in total harmony with the needs of imperialism and on the other, is in total antagonism to the struggle for liberation. The aim of such colonial education is to bring up a partly developed native only fit for brute labor, a native who has internalized a consciousness that blinds him into not seeing the loot and the plunder going on around him.

But such colonial education has another aim: to produce a native elite which has absorbed the culture of imperialism, and through whom imperialism, in its neocolonial stages, con continue looting and plundering the wealth of the country.

Neocolonialism is that process in which a country is nominally independent but its economy is still in the hands of the imperialist bourgeoisie. Nothing has, in substance, changed. The only change is that where before the imperialist bourgeoisie used to exploit through its settler or

Education for a National Culture

feudal representatives in the colonized territory, now it does so through a native bourgeoisie nurtured in the racial womb of colonialism but now eternally grateful for being allowed to raise a flag and to join Europeans in looting and plundering now that the racial barriers to property accumulation have been removed.

The native bourgeoisie which takes the flag at independence has been very well described by Frantz Fanon in that brilliant chapter titled "Pitfalls of National Consciousness" in his book *The Wretched of the Earth*. It's a chapter which should be compulsory reading for all newly independent countries who want to opt for a different path of development. The chapter will serve as a warning of what not to be since the picture it draws correctly describes the situation in most independent African countries:

> The national middle class which takes over power at the end of the colonial regiment is an underdeveloped class. It has practically no economic power, and in any case it is in no way commensurate with the bourgeoisie of the mother country whom it hopes to replace. In its wilful narcissism, the national middle class is easily convinced that it can advantageously replace the middle class of the mother country. But that same independence which literally drives it into a corner will give rise within its ranks to catastrophic reactions, and will oblige it to send out frenzied appeals for help to the former mother country. The university and merchant classes which make up the most enlightened section of the new state are in fact characterized by the smallness of their number and their being concentrated in the capital, and the type of activities in which they are engaged: business, agriculture and liberal professions. Neither financiers nor industrial magnates are to be found within this national middle class. The national bourgeoisie of underdeveloped countries is not engaged in production, nor in invention, nor labor; it is completely canalized into activities of the intermediary type. Its innermost vocation seems to be to keep in the running and to be part of the racket. The psychology of the national bourgeoisie is that of the businessman, not that of a captain of industry . . .

Fanon goes on to describe the various characteristics of this class which wants to follow the Western bourgeoisie along its path of negation and decadence.

> Because it is bereft of ideas, because it lives to itself and cuts itself off from the people, undermined by its hereditary incapacity to think in terms of all the problems of the nation as seen from the point of view of the whole nation, the national middle class will have nothing better to do than to take on the role of manager for Western enterprise, and it will in practice set up its country as the brothel of Europe.

This petit-bourgeoisie can play that role without seeing any contradiction because, in the colonial stage, they had completely imbibed the culture of slavery and hence a slave consciousness and world outlook.

During the neocolonial stage of imperialism education and culture play an even more important role as instruments of domination and oppression. European naming systems; European language; European theater; European literature; European content in teaching materials; all these areas, so central to culture, are left intact. Since the petit-bourgeoisie grew up accepting the world-view of the imperialist bourgeoisie, it will drive the youth even more vigorously into educational factories producing the same world-view. More churches are built, religious programs on radio or television are intensified. This class wants to prove to its Western mentors that it is civilized, that it is cultured, that it will not bring chaos into the country; it will try to prove that all the former accusations of inability to run the country were false. The moment this class accepts the imperialist bourgeois terms of evaluation of what constitutes progress, civilization, stability and so on, the imperialist bourgeoisie has won the battle and the war. For the Western imperialist bourgeoisie, civilization, stability, progress, mean the continuation of the colonial state, the colonial economic structure, with, of course, a few cosmetic reforms (like allowing a few natives to own farms, businesses, and go to live and drink in places that were formerly for whites only) to deceive the populace.

A petit-bourgeoisie which refuses to negate its roots in Western education and culture, develops into what Fanon describes as "a little greedy caste, avid and voracious, with the mind of a huckster, only too glad to accept the dividends that the former colonial power hands out to it. This get-rich-quick middle class shows itself incapable of great ideas or of inventiveness. It remembers what it has read in European textbooks and imperceptibly it becomes, not even the replica of Europe, but its caricature."

Now a people who want total liberation must recognize imperialism under European, Japanese or American guise, as the main enemy. They must recognize the two stages of imperialism, colonial and neocolonial, and accept the full implications of that recognition. That means that the battle is not won with its flag and a national anthem. The aim of imperialism whether in its colonial or neocolonial stage is to steal the wealth generated by the people: that is generated by the labor power of the workers and peasants of the colonial world. Imperialism aims at economic control, that is the control of the productive forces of that country. The political and cultural institutions it sets up are only to facilitate this theft and robbery. Therefore for as long as the economy of the country is not liberated, that is for as long as the wealth of the land does not go back to feed, clothe and shelter those whose labor power produced it, those people cannot consider themselves free and liberated.

A people engaged in the struggle for liberation must then recognize that the content of that liberation is the liberation of that economy from foreign and internal parasites. Any reform in education and culture must keep that objective clear in mind if such reforms are going to be useful and relevant. The aim is to devise an education system that not only gives people a true knowledge of their relations to nature and to other men, but which imparts a culture that embodies a consciousness, an ideological world outlook and value system that is a complete negation of imperialist culture, value systems, and world outlook.

If the colonial and neocolonial education aimed at imparting a culture of the partly developed individual who only vaguely understands the forces at work in society, an individual who is weak in body, feeble in mind, cowardly and subservient in spirit in face of an exploiter and oppressor, then an education for liberation ought to aim at producing a fully developed individual who understands the forces at work in society, an individual imbued with great hatred of all parasitic relationships of exploitation and oppression, an individual imbued with great patriotic pride and courage, an individual desirous of a total control of his natural and social environment.

This can only be achieved by the kind of education described by Marx as polytechnic education. Such an education system would have three aims:

(1) Provision of mental education. This would aim at developing the mental capacities of the people. People should be taught their history, their art, their literature, their theater, their dances first before being taught other people's cultural achievements. Their history, art, literature, theater, dances should be interpreted from the point of view of the needs of the majority: the workers and peasants. In this context, political education is crucial. By this I don't mean education for conformity but a political education that raises people's awareness and particularly their awareness of the social forces at work. This education should endow a people with a scientific understanding of the laws governing nature and society: that is, endow them with a scientific understanding of the world. But it is to understand it in order to change it!

(2) Provision of physical education. This would aim at producing healthy strong individuals. This would produce vigorous minds and bodies fully prepared in their twin struggle with nature and with other men. This would include everything from the simplest gymnastic to military training. A people must be in a position to defend the gains of their history and revolutionary changes. The whole people should be in a state of military preparedness to defend their revolution. A standing army should only be the highest concentrated expression of the military preparedness of the whole people.

(3) Economic and technological education through involvement in production. Everybody ought to be involved in productive labor. Every child

should be taught some technological skill that would enable him or her to engage in direct productive labor. The aim should be to turn everybody into a producer, so that the nation eventually becomes an association of producers who are masters of their natural and social environment. The aim is to produce a producer, a thinker and a fighter all integrated in the same individual.

What then I am advocating is not just education and culture per se. I am calling for an education for a national patriotic culture to produce fully developed individuals with a consciousness that man must be the master of both natural nature and his social nature. Education and culture should not only explain the world but must prepare the recipients to change the world. Man is the creator of his destiny and we, as an African people, can only get the destiny we create for ourselves.

I would like to end this address with the closing words of Frantz Fanon in his book *The Wretched of the Earth:*

> Comrades, let us not pay tribute to Europe by creating states, institutions and societies which draw their inspiration from her.
>
> Humanity is waiting for something other from us than such imitations which would be almost an obscene caricature.
>
> If we want to turn Africa into a New Europe . . . then let us leave the destiny of our countries to Europeans. They will know how to do it better than the most gifted among us.
>
> But if we want humanity to advance a step further, if we want to bring it up to a different level than that which Europe has shown it, then we must invent and we must make discoveries.
>
> If we wish to live to our people's expectations, we must seek the response elsewhere than in Europe.
>
> Moreover, if we wish to reply to the expectations of the people of Europe, it is no good sending them back a reflection, even an ideal reflection, of their society and their thoughts with which from time to time they feel immeasurably sickened.
>
> For Europe, for ourselves and for humanity, comrades, we must turn over a new leaf, we must work out new concepts, and try to set foot a new man.

Frantz Fanon should of course have specified that by Europe he means imperialist (capitalist) Europe, and that seeking responses elsewhere means the working class and the peasantry seeking liberation in a different higher social system of democracy and socialism which can only be brought about by the overthrow of the rule of imperialism and its comprador class allies in Africa.

Friends, before the Portuguese intervention, Zimbabwe used to be the seat of a great African civilization with an architecture our detractors still try to explain away. Today, in the latter quarter of the 20th century, there's no reason why Zimbabwe should not be the seat of a new beginning for the final homecoming of the new man of Africa. Our educational system and culture should and must be geared towards the homecoming of the New African.

But the New African will not be given us. He will be a product of intense revolutionary class struggle led by a revolutionary party of workers and peasants, at all levels: economic, political, cultural and ideological.

---

*This paper was first given at the Zimbabwean Seminar on Education held in Harare, in August 1981. It was subsequently published as a pamphlet by Zimbabwe Publishing House.

Kimathi's Will

KIMATHI: In the court of Imperialism!
There has never and will never be
Justice for the people
Under imperialism.
Justice is created
through a revolutionary struggle
Against all the forces of imperialism.
Our struggle must therefore continue,
our people will never surrender.
Internal and external foes
will be demolished
And Kenya shall be free!
So, go!
Organize in your homes
Organize in the mountains
Know that your only
Kindred blood is he
who is in the struggle
Denounce those who weaken
Our struggle
by creating ethnic divisions
Uproot from you those
Who are selling out to imperialism
Kenyan masses shall be free!

From *The Trial of Dedan Kimathi*

The Voice of the Kenyan People

We are not afraid of detention
Or of being locked in prisons
Or of being deported to remote islands
Because we shall never cease
To struggle and fight for liberation
Until our country is free!

You traitors who love foreign things and luxuries
Remember that these things cannot be equal to our country,
And they will never satisfy your stomachs.
This country is ours,
Our own inheritance from Ngai,
It is ours for ever and ever.

From *Thunder from the Mountains*

When evil doing comes like falling rain

The first time it was reported that our friends were being butchered there was a cry of horror. Then a hundred were butchered. But when a thousand were butchered and there was no end to the butchery, a blanket of silence spread.
When evil-doing comes like falling rain, nobody calls out "stop."
When crimes begin to pile up they become invisible.

An exerpt from a poem by Bertolt Brecht